MOMENTS
of GRACE

MOMENTS
of GRACE

Days of a
Faith-Filled Dreamer

Christopher de Vinck

Foreword by Ronald Rolheiser

Paulist Press
New York/Mahwah, NJ

Jacket art by Cindy Woods. Used by permission of her estate.

I'd like to thank the following publications where portions of this book first appeared: *Wall Street Journal*, *Good Housekeeping*, *Reader's Digest*, *National Catholic Reporter*, and especially the New Jersey *Bergen Record* and its Op-Ed editor, Peter Grad.

Unless otherwise noted, the scripture quotations outlined herein are from the New Revised Standard Version Bible, copyright © 1989 by the Division of Christian Education of the National Council of Churches of Christ in the U.S.A. Used by permission.

Jacket design by Sharyn Banks
Book design by Lynn Else

Library of Congress Cataloging-in-Publication Data

De Vinck, Christopher, 1951–
   Moments of grace : days of a faith-filled dreamer / Christopher de Vinck.
     p. cm.
   ISBN 978-0-8091-0597-7 (alk. paper)
   1. De Vinck, Christopher, 1951– I. Title.
   BX4705.D473A3 2011
   204'.4092—dc22
   [B]
   2011004643

Published by Paulist Press
997 Macarthur Boulevard
Mahwah, New Jersey 07430

www.paulistpress.com

Printed and bound in the
United States of America

"Write it on your heart that every day is the best day in the year."
—Ralph Waldo Emerson

CONTENTS

FOREWORD

Ronald Rolheiser

Seventeen years ago, I was killing time in an airport bookstore when I picked up a copy of Christopher de Vinck's *Only the Heart Knows How to Find Them: Precious Memories for a Faithless Time*. I had been struck by the book's title, and it came as advertised. It was a series of essays about his marriage, his wife, and his children: memories made precious by the way they were picked up and honored by a sensitive eye and an even more sensitive heart.

A year or so later, teaching an evening course in morality and religion at a state university, I assigned the book as required reading for a section of the course on sexuality and marriage. A young woman in the class, handing in her term paper at the end of the semester, made this comment: "You know, Father, I come from a pretty experiential background. Beginning in high school and right through my undergraduate years at college, I've slept my way through a couple of states. I always thought that this was some kind of liberation, a freedom from the morality of my parents. But reading Christopher's book made me realize something: *I want what he has!* I want that kind of love, that kind of family, that kind of home!" There were tears in her eyes as she shared this.

All of Christopher's books, including this one, might well be put under one title: *Precious Insights Emanating from a Sensitive Heart*. But their power, the power to move a jaded heart to a desire for new innocence, comes not just from his sensitivity. There are plenty of sensitive writers out there. His power comes from something else.

What is more unique, more precious, in Christopher is a rare combination of art and innocence. He's ever the sophisticated artist, and he is ever the person whose innocence belies our common conception of artists. He is innocent, but never naive; intelligent, but never cynical; rich in experience, but never jaded; simple, but never simplistic. He is deeply committed in his faith and his marriage, and struggles through all the tortured complexity of those areas. He is the type of person who can make a lifelong commitment, sweat blood, keep that commitment, and still fall in love every hour. All of this shows through in these essays. Complexity and idealism, often polar opposites, work together to make these writings rich.

De Vinck is also a gifted, careful writer. These essays, totally independent of their moral content, are simply very good pieces of writing. He is a craftsman, a diamond cutter who puts on microscopic glasses when he sits at his keyboard. These essays aren't tossed off: every word is cut and polished. Few spiritual writers write with as much literary talent and as much care for the literary quality of what they are doing.

Moments of Grace: Days of a Faith-Filled Dreamer can do for each of us what his book *Only the Heart Knows How to Find Them* did for that young woman whom I quoted above. These essays can help reawaken our souls to a deeper dream inside us, a dream of being clothed with the sun despite anything that's happened in our past, a dream of being enough inside our own skins so as see the sunset, taste our coffee, know more fully the love of those around us, and not have an excuse to absent ourselves when we finally find ourselves in God's presence.

Ronald Rolheiser
San Antonio, Texas
August 24, 2010

Autumn

The year's last, loveliest smile…

—William Cullen Bryant

SEPTEMBER 1

"Hope" is the thing with feathers.

—Emily Dickinson

I woke up this morning with a vague notion of regret, recognizing that I am limited in my choices, feeling annoyed that the carpenter bees are still embedded in the eaves of my house, and remembering what it was like to be twenty-three-years old.

Then I realized, as I stretched in bed, that I was shivering. For the first time in four months, the room was cold. Since May, the bedroom window has been open, allowing spring and summer air to ooze through the screen like ghosts, carrying with them the scent of spring flowers, the symphony of night crickets, and the low hum of air-conditioning units from the neighbors' homes.

But this morning, through the invisible network of a Canadian air mass, word was spreading, perhaps, to bears and badgers and a sixty-year-old man under the covers in his New Jersey home that autumn was once again upon us.

We build a life, gather books and furniture, arrange our homes in neat little rows, surround them with carpets of grass. If we live in the cities, we put up shelves, covet the windows with a view, manage to use every inch of space in our apartments, and relish our luck if a room contains direct sunlight during part of the day.

And yet, no matter how careful we are to buy the right couch or maintain the furnace, no matter how much we try to keep order in our homes, there is the slow and persistent power of ruin that pervades all that we do. If I do not vacuum the floors and wipe the tables and shelves in the house at least once a week, there will be a quick accumulation of dust that will coat the books, the carpets, the lampshades—and the house will quickly look like a portion of a ghost town.

If I don't wash the bathtub and dump green liquid into the drain, within a few weeks the tub will clog and resemble a mud hole.

I sometimes dare myself not to shave for two days, perhaps even a third day. I look in the mirror and see a man slowly turning into an old man. Everything, it seems, needs to be protected against the inevitability of impermanence and disintegration.

I woke up this morning feeling cold, recognizing that September means a shift in seasons, and that everything turns into dust, and I was depressed.

Nothing on this earth will retain its original shape. Everything is made of atoms and molecules, and how closely packed these atoms and molecules are will determine how long they will endure.

A rock in the backyard will last longer than my autographed copy of Harper Lee's novel, *To Kill a Mockingbird*. When we die, we will quickly disintegrate because we are so loosely held together. Our bones are strung with thin ligaments and muscles. Our hearts are thin little sacs that will dissolve like a paper bag in the rain. Our eyes are soft, little orbs that will dry out like prunes.

I do not want to die. I do not want to dry up like a mummy and disintegrate into dust. I don't want my bones to become brittle and melt into the ground and disappear.

I want to unfurl like a new rose and exude the perfume of my soul and attract women and ride horses in Texas. I'd like to read *The Great Gatsby* again for the first time, stand next to my wife Roe, and watch our children being born all over again.

I believe, sometimes, that evidence of eternity is hidden in the past. We are given examples of joy, memories that heal our wounds and soothe us with laughter, or with the nostalgia of knowing that what was once grand in our lives contains little seeds of hope that we can have those days again, or at least that those days once existed.

As I dressed this morning, I stepped up to the open window and inhaled the autumn air. Like great bellows, our lungs pull in the oxygen that, in part, sustains our bodies. I closed my eyes, considered gratitude for another morning, for another autumn season, and then I walked downstairs and opened the front door of the house to hunt for the newspaper.

As I stepped out of the house, I saw a squirrel's tail sticking up out of the pumpkin I had bought at the farmer's market and placed on the stoop the week before.

The squirrel had bored a hole into the pumpkin and was, headfirst, mining the seeds embedded inside its belly. When the squirrel heard me, its tail disappeared completely inside the pumpkin. I stood in silence, and then slowly the squirrel poked its head out of the hole. It looked at me. I looked at it. The squirrel's face was wet from pumpkin goo. It wrinkled its nose, chewed a bit on a pumpkin seed, and then wiggled out and sat on the top of the Halloween gourd.

I wrinkled my nose. The squirrel shook its tail a few times in anger or distress, then leaped onto the ground and disappeared up into the maple tree.

I bent over the pumpkin, reached into the hole the squirrel had created, and scooped out eight, flat pumpkinseeds. I looked at the white seeds on my flat palm, each containing biological threads that can be woven into pumpkins. Each seed was the possibility of a new universe, the replication of autumn and squirrels and old men bending down in the morning and considering the seeds like magic beans.

Like Jack in "Jack and the Beanstalk," I took the eight seeds, walked to the back of my house, and planted them behind the shed, hoping to create my own autumn next season, believing that we live with the evidence of cycles: winter, spring, summer, fall, and so to winter again.

Perhaps in the patterns of our lives we find hidden evidence of that magic thread that will bend like strands of DNA, that will zoom faster than Albert Einstein's theories and bring us to a future, a hidden crack in our graves, that will lead us to a place where we can open the door and breathe in the comfort of ordinary salvation.

There is hope in going out alone and gathering the seeds of the pumpkin.

SEPTEMBER 13

...the magic of wonder...

—Loren Eiseley

As I stepped out of the car and slowly walked up the stairs to the building where I work, I noticed that my left, brown shoe was untied. The lace dangled and flopped on the ground. That is when I noticed that my right shoe was black.

I work in a high school with over 3,200 teenagers who consider what you wear far more important than the state of the economy or global warming, and here I was, entering the building with a brown shoe on my left foot, and a black shoe on my right.

That morning, as I watched the television for headlines and for the day's weather, I had fumbled under the coffee table for my shoes. It was 6:15 in the morning; the shades were drawn; the day was overcast. I slipped into my shoes just as the reporter announced more suicide bombings in Iraq. I did not notice that I was wearing two different shoes.

A teacher shook her head when she saw my sartorial error and whispered, "Einstein." It is true. Albert Einstein was known for his eccentric style of dress, often coming to class in rumpled clothes, using a tie as a belt, or not wearing socks. He was known to call his wife when he was on a lecture tour and ask her where he was and what he was doing that day. It is easy, even for us mortal souls of average intelligence, to not notice common customs when we are distracted or tired, and yet when such silliness jumps at us, we laugh and we are delighted.

How easy it is to forget the child's ability to be dazzled. A tree is the world's tallest weed, and yet, when was the last time anyone took notice of the oak in the backyard? A bicycle is an extraordinary invention with spinning wheels and gears, a mini-universe controlled by a chain and brakes. Just a bicycle. Has anyone recently celebrated the window screen, or the sun?

Once, long ago, entire civilizations built the foundations of their religious beliefs on sun worship. Ra was the sun god in old Egypt. The pharaoh was considered the son of Ra. The Greeks had two sun gods: Apollo and Helios.

We wear sunglasses, and scientists destroyed the myth of the sun, telling us that it is about 70 percent hydrogen, 28 percent helium, and 2 percent combined gases. Once considered a power worthy of temples and adoration, the sun, we now know, is an ordinary star, one of more than 100 billion stars in our galaxy. No one notices any longer.

Place anything in the usual routine of our lives, and we eventually lose interest. An elephant in the zoo? Just an elephant. Shrug. The ocean? Water. Yawn.

Loren Eiseley, one of my favorite writers, wrote in his wonderful book *The Unexpected Universe*, "Today we know that the heart untouched by the magic of wonder may come to an impoverished age." We are a culture slowly surrendering our independent sense of glee to television cameras and to public-relation firms determined to *tell* us what is beautiful, smart, stylish, and amazing. We *are* slipping into an impoverished age if we allow others to manipulate our soul-self as they try to dull our abilities to know joy and beauty and delight when we see it.

Last week my wife and I visited my mother and father. When we returned, as we walked into the house, I gave the dog a biscuit and casually looked out the window to the backyard.

"Roe!" I called. "Look at that!"

Roe joined me at the kitchen window as we both considered the enormous tree branch that filled a quarter of the yard. We walked outside, down the deck, and onto the grass. I pointed up to the tree. "See how the tree is split in half? And look at all this bark scattered on the lawn. The tree was hit by lightning! This is just so great!"

The neighbors confirmed my suspicion.

"I saw the fireball," Patty said.

"You should have heard the explosion." The neighbor's son nearly sang with excitement. "I could smell the burning wood."

I turned to Roe and said, "I am so disappointed. I missed it. I would have like to have been here. We will never have a tree in our yard hit by lightning again, and I missed it."

We rush out of our houses to survey the damage done to a tree struck by lightning. We take notice of the size of the fallen branch and admire the scar in the tree, but by the end of the next day, the fallen tree is removed, and we all return to our houses. News over. Storm over. Lightning passed.

I like the flash of lightning. I like going to the zoo and seeing the elephant. Did you know that elephants show explicit joy when a calf has been born, or when they are playing games or greeting a friend? I like standing at the lip of the ocean and feeling a bit frightened.

We need to nurture our gift of awe. We need to remember how to react to the world the way we did when we were children.

I liked walking the halls of the high school that day in my brown and black shoes. We need to be a bit more eccentric.

"Once you can accept the universe as matter expanding into nothing that is something," Einstein once said, "wearing stripes with plaid comes easy."

We live in a world that is constantly moving from nothing to something. The thing is that we have to notice the movement and recognize there is something there after all: elephants, the sun, funny clothes, lightning, and flying bark.

SEPTEMBER 14

...all dreams of the soul...
—William Butler Yeats

After work one day, many years ago, one of my colleagues and I were walking to our cars in the parking lot when he said, without any provocation, "Yep. Kids are gone. Dog's dead."

Brad was in his midfifties, balding, already a bit worn out, and I felt sorry for him. He tried to explain to me how much he didn't enjoy his empty nest; how he looked at his wife and she just looked back and handed him the TV guide. "I don't know what to do with myself when I get home. How many times can I paint the house?"

Brad's four children were successful adults and on their own.

"I go to bed at night and sometimes peek in their rooms just to see if by chance they are in their beds, dreaming about the upcoming little league game, or looking forward to buying the dog they saw at the pet shop."

Now *I* am sixty, balding, a bit worn out, but I am determined to rearrange the sticks in my empty nest so that I can continue to live a fulfilling life, so that I can face the challenges of the last years of my existence with hope and joy.

It is often said in politics that candidates lack "the vision thing." If we allow our loneliness and doubts to overwhelm us, if we regret the loss of our past, we can easily lose ourselves in soap operas and restaurants; we can thumb through photo albums with sorrow, share our physical aches and pains with our friends, and live a life filled with card games and crossword puzzles as we attempt to numb ourselves into death.

But if we have a vision about passion, beauty, goodness; if we learn the joys of compromise, acceptance, and certitude; if we see old age not as fading memories, but as a vibrant new day filled with surprises—we will live out the rest of our lives in stubborn dignity.

When I was a child, when the wind was up and the shutters banged against the house, I imagined that I could fly. I pretended that if I spread open my beige coat like wings, a rush from the sky would pick me up as if I were a kite, and I'd rise above the lawn and the chicken coop. I pretended that my house spun under me like a falling leaf as I flew to Japan. (It was my notion as a child that Japan and flight were connected somehow: paper cranes, lanterns, mist, and dragons.)

I've had a recurring flying dream at least five times in my life. I fly with my daughter as she laughs, holding an umbrella. Once we flew with an antelope. A dream world is the place where we go when we are filled with doubt, when the routine is dull or confusing, or when we are tired and we need a sudden jolt of fantasy or monsters to stir up our sense of relief for normalcy.

Now at the end of another season, at the end of our youth, all seems to be collapsing. The flowers fade like dying dancers, drooping over in a last bow, and the stage of the garden is bare and empty.

This afternoon, I rescued one pot of red-and-white impatiens and dragged it into this small room where I write. It now leans against the French door that separates it from the dead plants and the cold.

How long can I preserve late August in this room where I write, where the sun is warm and there is no frost?

Flowers possess the combined nature of life and death: life so sudden in its vibrant colors and soft petals, and death equally sudden in ice or lack of moisture. The ancient Greeks and Romans always wore crowns of flowers at their festivals and, with equal gravity, sprinkled the petals of flowers on the graves of their loved ones. Flowers represent the miraculous nature of what can happen given enough light and water, and they speak in silence at the aroma of death.

I know of a college professor who once said to his students at an all-women's school, "If you come to class tomorrow wearing flowers in your hair, I will give you all A's for the course." The next day, all the young women sat in class with a single rose in their braids and tresses.

Last Halloween the doorbell had rung and there stood our neighbor and her two-year-old daughter dressed as Dorothy from *The Wizard of Oz*. The girl wore a blue polka-dot dress and ruby slippers; her hair was beautifully woven into French braids. After she reached into the bowl for her bit of candy, she had said, "Thank-you," with grace and ease, and then she stepped into the house. Her mother was a bit embarrassed as Roe and I said, "Oh, that is perfectly fine. Wonderful. Let her come in." The little girl walked inside the living room, patted the head of our dog, and then stepped into the den and found a Mickey Mouse plush doll on the shelf. She ran to the toy, hugged it, and said, "Mickey Mouse!"

When the little girl and her mother had walked away down the leaf-covered street, I turned to Roe and whispered, "I'd like a granddaughter like her someday."

How best do we define the dreams that we collect along the way? When we were children, I remember how my older brother and I baked apples in the woods. We ran to the apple tree in the backyard and picked out the fattest apples we could find. He showed me how to core the center of the apple and pack it with brown sugar, then we wrapped the apples in aluminum foil. "Come on, Chrissy," he said, and we ran to the middle of the woods where he had made, many years earlier, a campfire pit rimmed with stones. We gathered sticks and leaves around our raw apples, then my brother lit the fire, and we sat side by side and watched the yellow flames glow against each other's face. It was best to bake apples in the dark.

After a while, we reached into the smoke with two sticks and pulled out our two apples. They were hot. Steam rose through the slits in the aluminum foil. We broke open the wrapping, then, after a few minutes, we each took a bite from our sugar-filled apples, and all of autumn and juice and sugar and time and dreams covered our tongues and cheeks. Who could say that we were not the lords of the forest?

Dreams are nothing more than a taste for what is beyond the natural world. The little girl from Oz floated in and out of the house, bringing us a message of grace and delight. The baked apples oozed melting brown sugar from another universe.

The writer W. B. Yeats, in his poem "The Phases of the Moon," wrote: "All dreams of the soul end in a beautiful man's or woman's body."

While I am heavy with the day's labor, while I have my

doubts, I am light in my dreaming, which is why, as I sleep, it is easy to fly at night through the mist on a Japanese paper crane.

The children may be gone, and the dog may be dead, but watch with me how long the flowers will last in my heated room. Ride with my daughter and me on the back of the wild antelope as we all dream of our souls floating away in autumn.

SEPTEMBER 15

I shall hear in heaven.

—Ludwig van Beethoven

When I was in graduate school at Columbia University, the student who occupied the room next to mine owned one record album: horn concertos by George Philip Telemann. I do not remember his name. He had a bristly mustache, wire-framed glasses, a thin face; we never spoke, except to say hello when we passed each other in the hallway of the graduate dorm. But each night, at around 9:30, these regal trumpets emanated through the thick wall that separated my room from the Telemann enthusiast.

I didn't mind. I'd sprawl out on my bed and listen to the distant music. Sometimes I'd fall asleep and wake up in the middle of the night to the roar of city traffic, or to the garbage truck swallowing trash from the green dumpster that sat in the alley below my second-story window.

I cannot sleep with a ticking clock. I cannot sleep with a window air conditioner. For the first three years of our marriage, Roe would chuckle as, just before we went to bed, I stopped the old school clock we had bought at an antique shop, and restarted the pendulum's swing in the morning, just so I would not hear the ticking, ticking, ticking, even though the clock was downstairs in the living room. Finally I just stopped the clock entirely, and it hasn't run in twenty-five years.

When our children were little, I liked checking on them before going to bed. I liked resting my arms on the baby's crib and listening to her breathe. I liked hearing the voice of my son whispering in the darkness, "Good night, Daddy."

For all of my life I have lived close enough to the train tracks that I could hear the trains clatter and the whistles blow.

I like the sound of the leaves brushing against themselves during an oncoming storm. I like Bing Crosby's voice, the music of Bach, the squawk of blue jays, the laugh of my daughter.

For ten years, I wrote in the basement of this little house, and each time the furnace kicked in, I flinched.

What is sound? How do we hear? Of course, we can know the mechanics of it all: the outer and inner ear, the vibrations, the ear drum, but there is more to sound than just anatomy.

A porpoise can send out clicks through the water. Birds, lions, wolves send out songs and roars. But a woman can whisper, "I love you." A monk can sing a Gregorian chant. We take for granted the pleasure of hearing.

Helen Keller wrote in a letter to a friend that "after a lifetime in silence and darkness...to be deaf is a greater affliction than to be blind. Hearing is the soul of knowledge and information of a high order. To be cut off from hearing is to be isolated indeed."

What do we do if we are slowly becoming deaf? My father, who is ninety-nine, tells stories about his day, enjoys crossword puzzles, roots for the Belgian tennis players on the television matches—and is nearly incapable of hearing anything anymore. He often feels isolated, sits in his chair during holiday celebrations and smiles, maintains his dignity, and sometimes speaks about his life as a young adult: sailing, riding horses, meeting my mother, coming to America, finding work.

Whenever I'd call home in the past and my father would answer the phone, I'd ask him how he was, and he answered, always, "Everything is under control."

My father does not answer the phone any longer. He cannot hear it ringing, and he cannot hear any voice speaking.

In the middle of the night, when I cannot sleep, I often think of my father lying in his bed in the silence of his room. I wish I could tell him that if he listens carefully, he can hear the cornets of Telemann penetrating the thick walls of the room. I wish I could remind my father how the morning lark sings.

I wish I could tell my father that my hearing is slowly deteriorating. I wish I could tell my father I am afraid to die.

SEPTEMBER 18

Constant attention by a good nurse may be just as important
as a major operation by a surgeon.

—Dag Hammarskjöld

Many years ago my young daughter, Karen, woke up in the middle of a Saturday night with severe pain in her right foot.

"Mommy, it hurts so much."

I vaguely heard the commotion as I slid back into sleep.

The next morning, Roe spoke about Karen's difficult night with the pain in her foot. "Perhaps someone ought to look at it."

Our regular doctor didn't have Sunday-morning hours, so we thought it best to take Karen to the emergency facility on the highway. Twenty minutes later, I carried my daughter into the lobby of the small brick building. After Roe and I filled out some forms, we were quickly introduced to a young doctor. X-rays of the foot were taken.

"A simple bone chip," the doctor pointed out. "I am not qualified to wrap the foot. You'll need to see an orthopedic surgeon. He'll know if she needs a soft or hard cast."

Two days afterward, Roe stepped into the orthopedic surgeon's office with Karen and the X-rays.

After the new doctor examined Karen's foot and looked at the films, he said to Roe, "There is something more here. It isn't a bone chip. The first doctor's diagnosis is an honest mistake. You see here?" The surgeon pointed it out to my wife. "This does look like a chip on the bone, but it is really quite normal."

Roe looked at the black-and-gray film illuminated against the light.

"But look here," the doctor continued. "Do you see this bone? It is much larger than the others in her foot. That concerns me."

And so began the very first time any of our children was threatened by a force beyond a mother and father's protection.

"What does it mean?" Roe asked.

"I'd like to order some tests on Karen: a bone scan, a blood test, and an MRI."

"But what does it mean?"

"Well, that bone. It is abnormally large. There's a reason: an infection, a fracture, perhaps a tumor. These tests will begin to tell us more."

The tests told us more. The MRI indicated that her bone was not broken. The blood test didn't detect an infection. But the bone scan pointed to the flare-up of pain in Karen's foot, and after three weeks of tests, the orthopedic surgeon looked at the results and urged us to take her to the Sloan-Kettering Cancer Center in New York City.

I will never forget the image of nine-year-old Karen walking through the hospital doors, clutching the large X-ray envelope against her chest.

"We really can't tell what is going on in Karen's foot at the moment," the new doctor told us after examining the X-rays. "She will have to have a biopsy."

I thought a biopsy would be a simple needle inserted into the bone.

"I'd like to admit Karen on Monday," the doctor said. "I'll perform the surgery on Tuesday morning, and if all goes well, Karen can go home on Wednesday."

"Excuse me," I said. "What did you say? Karen will have to stay overnight?"

Not until I was home and Karen was in bed did I fully understand what was happening. The doctors suspected that Karen had cancer.

We live our lives in the rhythms of drama, between ordinary routines and sudden jolts. I had thought until this point in my life that I could protect my children.

The poet Derek Walcott said that he liked growing up in the Caribbean. Living so close to the sea as a child, he said, gave him a sense of things larger than he was out there, things vast and powerful.

There is no power on this earth greater than death. But I was still foolish enough, or young enough, to believe I could fight death as it tried to press against my daughter. I was a madman, believing in my superior strength in opposition to so vast and powerful a thing, this cancer.

On the morning of the biopsy, an anesthesiologist stepped up to Karen's bed and placed a green surgical cap on my daughter's head. As Karen tucked her long brown hair under the cap, the doctor told her she looked like a fashion model.

The only thing Karen had wanted to bring to the hospital

was Penny, her new Disney Dalmatian plush dog with its pink nametag. Penny traveled with Karen through the admissions office. Penny sat on Karen's lap when the intravenous tube was thrust into her vein.

Just as the nurse began to push Karen toward the operating room, my wife reached over to take the stuffed animal, for we'd been told our daughter couldn't have anything with her during surgery.

"Oh, Karen can take Penny," said the nurse, with a beautiful Dutch accent.

As Karen was wheeled away from us, she waved, Penny tucked under her arm.

We all endure hints of anguish differently. I wanted to stop the play, send the director to lunch, take Roe and Karen home, and forget the whole thing. I was able to teach Karen how to ride a bicycle. I was able to comfort her when she had a fever. I wasn't able to take her away from the surgeons.

Roe and I spent the longest two hours of our lives sitting together in the hospital lobby as we waited to hear the biopsy results.

The morning sun leaned against us.

Finally, down the hall, I could see, in the hospital crowd, our doctor in his green surgical gown.

"It looks good. I saw no evidence of cancer, no evidence of a tumor or an infection. I think it is a stress fracture. The bone in her foot sustained a trauma of some sort. The bone is bent and her body thinks it is broken, so her immune system is simply trying to repair the supposed damage. We couldn't tell this without the biopsy. She's going to be fine."

Roe and I were allowed to be with Karen right after the surgery. Our daughter was curled up under a blanket. A mist of steam was being pumped around her face.

"Is she all right?" I asked the nurse.

"She's fine. She's just waking up. The steam helps her. The doctor said your daughter is fine. We don't get much good news in this recovery room."

I pulled Karen's blanket over her bare shoulders, and there, on the other side of her little bed, I found Penny, wearing a green surgical mask and cap.

Roe and I celebrate and sing that Karen didn't have cancer. We human beings ought to celebrate and sing in praise of men and women who devote their lives to a career so filled with stress, sadness, and sometimes joy, such as those at Sloan-Kettering.

We can be grateful for the development of scientific research and discoveries, but let us not forget that someone took the time to tie a little hat and mask around a toy dog, just so a child could wake up and smile, no matter what the outcome of her test.

Vast and powerful indeed.

SEPTEMBER 22

A society without religion is like a vessel without a compass.
—Napoleon Bonaparte

I received news that my aunt died. She and my uncle knew each other since they were teenagers. They had one son, lived quiet lives: he as a banker, and she as a housewife and mother. Two years ago, their son—my cousin—died of a massive heart attack the day after Easter. I believe my aunt never regained her strength from the shock of her loss.

Uncle Henri lives in Belgium in a high-rise apartment complex. He lives in one of the upper floors that overlook the city where he was born and where he has spent his entire life. He said on the phone to my mother, "I am all alone now. It is just me and the dog. I wish I had a little garden. I do not know what to do."

What do we say to someone who has lost his way? When I visited Belgium for the first time, I stayed at my aunt and uncle's home. As I stepped out of the house on the first morning to take a walk in the village, my uncle said to me, "If you get lost, just look for the steeple, and you'll find your way back home. The steeple is always in the center of the village."

I felt the same thing whenever I visited the financial district in New York City. I could always find my way because, at that time before 9/11, I could see the Twin Towers of the World Trade Center no matter where I was.

We seek markers along the way to keep us on track. In the fairy tale, Hansel and Gretel knew where they were coming from by dropping little bright pebbles as they walked, so that they could find their way back home. With the new technology, we can now click onto our computers and see our house from a satellite photograph. There are handheld devices where we can locate every space on the planet.

The house where I grew up was situated on a hill, and I could see the house in the background no matter where I played: in the woods as we built campfires; across the frozen swamp as we ice-skated in midwinter; from the neighbor's house as we played stickball. I always felt as if that house was my beacon, always out there, just beyond the sandbox or just beyond the pine trees, always there, always pulling me back in the evening.

Some years ago, a beluga whale swam eighty miles off course from the ocean. It was discovered miles and miles up the Delaware River. News helicopters recorded live pictures of the whale pushing itself to the surface, and then flicking its tail in a steady rhythm. Commuter trains stopped so passengers could admire the whale. People lined the sides of the river to observe the sea creature. Whale cookies were quickly created by the local baker and sold briskly. The ice-cream store created "beluga flavored" ice cream, which was really vanilla ice cream with a new name, but no one cared. It sold briskly as well. The last report I heard stated that the whale was still confused, still lost in the river.

In my own life I trusted my own inner-guidance system when I met Roe for the first time. I just knew she was the one for me. I trusted myself when I knew that I had to make changes in my career. And sometimes, when I was lost, I needed extra guidance.

Eventually, the marine biologists with the National Oceanic and Atmospheric Administration captured the whale and sent it home.

I spent the afternoon today sitting on the back porch of my parents' home. It is the same house where I grew up. My mother is eighty-nine, and my father is ninety-nine, and they live in the same house on the hill. I can still find my way home.

We are given, throughout our lives, bright pebbles to drop behind us so that we can find our way back to our true selves, or to our childhoods, or to a place where we first were loved.

I called my uncle on the phone to extend my sorrow at the death of his wife. "I am all alone," he said. "I have nowhere to go," he nearly cried.

"Just look for the steeple, Uncle Henri. Just look for the steeple."

OCTOBER 1

A drowsy, dreamy influence seems to hang over the land...
—Washington Irving

There is, in a forgotten land, many Octobers ago, a place where a boy and a girl smeared their faces with charcoal and ran out the front door carrying white pillowcases that flapped in the still night like thin, little ghosts.

I was that boy, and the girl was my sister Anne. It was 1961, and I was ten years old, and she was twelve. I was a pirate and Anne was a cat. There was a chill, dew perhaps, spread out against the cornfields and alleyways that led to all the houses that sat like fat gods, dispensing Hershey's Bars and pennies for UNICEF.

Perhaps it was not the dew, but the moon's light that brushed against us, causing our skin to ripple with dimples.

I liked to kick the curled, stiff leaves as my sister and I walked side by side trading candy. "I'll give you two Snickers bars for your Turkish Taffy?" Deal. And then we raced to see who would be the first one to press the next illuminated doorbell.

"Well, well, what do we have here?" old Mrs. Coster asked, as she extended a bowl filled with homemade peanut brittle. Anne meowed and I shook my pirate sword. Mrs. Coster pretended that she did not recognize us, and just as Anne and I stepped away from the door, called out, "Give my love to your mother!" What mother? Old Mother Hubbard? Old Salem witch mother? Halloween mother? Mrs. Coster was not fooled.

There was always Patty and Johnny to catch up to, she in her princess dress and he in his Davy Crockett costume. He never let me wear his coonskin hat, but we partnered up just the same, covering the south side of town.

It was the moon, I thought at first, until I looked up again and saw the streetlight winking down between the trees—city eye, Halloween eye—and our long shadows trailed behind us like pet shrouds.

Candy corn, wax teeth, Tootsie Roll Pops, and Cracker Jack. Our pillowcases swelled and bulged; and Dr. Schultz gave out quarters; and Mrs. Short, marshmallow pumpkins.

Too soon we said goodbye to Johnny and Patty, and Anne and I turned back toward the house: October house, autumn house, that place where candy apples and cider sat on the kitchen table, and perhaps a skeleton or two hung from the trees, and bats swooped down, and somewhere a witch laughed, and a garbage can rattled down the street as it rolled and tumbled and turned into Johnny with his laughter and Patty with a shouted "Boo!" And we laughed and roared, "Happy Halloween" and "Trick or treat," and they closed their door and were home, and Anne and I made our way down our driveway with the stones crunching under our feet.

In Shakespeare's *Macbeth*, the first witch asks, "When shall we three meet again: in thunder, lightning, or in rain?" And the second witch answers, "When the hurly-burly's done, when the battle's lost and won."

I have fought the battle of lost youth for decades, and even after all the hurly-burly of my own life, I still think of Anne and me dressed in Halloween costumes, trading candy and laughing with old Mrs. Coster.

Washington Irving, in his famous little story "The Legend of Sleepy Hollow," wrote that "a drowsy, dreamy influence seems to hang over the land, and to pervade the very atmosphere."

For as long as I have been a writer, I have been trying to create something around me: a coat, a coffin, a suit of armor, the arms of a woman. It is difficult to tell from day to day, but when I was a child that dream influence was collected in white pillowcases, and home was just at the end of the stone driveway.

When shall we meet again, Anne? In thunder, lightning, or in rain?

OCTOBER 3

But I am done with apple-picking now.
Essence of winter sleep is on the night,
The scent of apples: I am drowsing off.

—Robert Frost

Autumn in New Jersey is just as charming, and just as robust, as autumn in New England. You just have to know exactly where to look, and exactly how to prepare yourself for the harvest moon and for the witch's arrival on Halloween.

As is our routine in the autumn season, a few weeks ago Roe and I drove to Warwick, New York, to pick apples. After collecting a bag of Red Delicious and McIntosh apples, we had a picnic on the orchard grass, and headed home.

As we reentered New Jersey, down through the northern tip of Sussex County, we came across a small, brown sign with black letters: Fresh Eggs. We drove by, and on second thought, we turned the car around, returned to the little sign, and pulled left into a narrow driveway. There, on a small hill, sat a small red barn like a happy rooster bathing in the afternoon sun. Outside the barn was a wide table filled with pumpkins and apple cider, and surrounded with pots of yellow and red chrysanthemums.

Roe wanted a dozen fresh eggs. I wanted a fat, orange pumpkin—to follow the poet John Greenleaf Whittier's suggestion. He was an influential Quaker writer of the 1800s, who in his poem "The Pumpkin" wrote about the "ugly faces we carved in its skin, glaring out through the dark with a candle within!"

The woman who owned the property walked out to greet us, and when we asked if there were any more eggs, she said, "Yes. I'll pull them from the nests and wash them for you." We spoke a bit: I saying that she had discovered paradise; she saying that she had six children, that her husband was a carpenter, and that she maintained the seasonal roadside stand as a hobby.

As the woman in her black boots and long, lovely hair walked to the henhouse, Roe and I stepped into the barn where there were haystacks and pumpkins, cornstalks and chrysanthemums, arranged just for the fun of it, it seemed, for the cover of the old *Saturday Evening Post*. On the barn door was a poster from the 1950s of an illuminated pumpkin that looked also like the moon.

The moon is a bright orange pumpkin in autumn, the harvest moon hanging in the darkness like a Japanese lantern on a stick, looming down on us. Each Halloween the street lights on our dark road, like little moons, guide trick-or-treaters up the narrow, concrete walk that leads to our front door. I like watching tiny hands reaching out of their devil or witch costumes as I offer a bowl filled with chocolate Milky Ways and Hershey's Bars.

Twenty years ago, when my daughter was five-years-old, she was a witch for Halloween. Roe sewed the costume, and searched the stores for just the right pointed hat. My favorite part of the costume was Karen's red sneakers visible under the long, black skirt decorated with moons and stars.

Perhaps the reason we like Halloween so much is because it is a day that reminds us of our own youth, when we could all pretend to be something other than who we were, when we could be a little mischievous, toss eggs, soap windows, and join

Huckleberry Finn and Tom Sawyer out behind the old school building, and smoke acorn pipes and feel just fine.

Whittier's poem "The Pumpkin" continues this way:

> When we laughed round the corn-heap, with hearts all
>   in tune,
> Our chair a broad pumpkin,—our lantern the moon,
> Telling tales of the fairy who travelled like steam
> In a pumpkin-shell coach, with two rats for her team!

It has been reported that New Jersey farmers experienced a bumper crop of pumpkins this year because of the heat and well-timed rainfall.

I like autumn and Halloween because it makes me think of paradise: a sumptuous roadside stand, the little sneakers in the attic that once fit my grown daughter, pumpkins on a doorsill.

In her famous novel *My Antonia*, the nineteenth-century American novelist Willa Cather wrote , "I was something that lay under the sun and felt it, like the pumpkins, and I did not want to be anything more. I was entirely happy. Perhaps we feel like that when we die and become a part of something entire, whether it is sun and air, or goodness and knowledge."

I like autumn in New Jersey because it make me feel happy, as if I am a part of something good as the cold air swirls around us and the apple cider is sweet.

OCTOBER 15

Contrary to all we hear about women and their empty-nest problem, it may be fathers more often than mothers who are pained by the children's imminent or actual departure—fathers who want to hold back the clock, to keep the children in the home for just a little longer. Repeatedly women compare their own relief to their husband's distress.

—Lillian Breslow Rubin

"Dad, can you help me with my English homework?"

"Daddy? Did you see my baseball mitt?"

"Dad, I need a ride home. Can you come get me?"

And so it was for twenty-three years: my children defining who I was in the house Roe and I had bought thirty years ago. I liked driving the children to the zoo. I liked driving Michael to fencing lessons. I liked reading *Treasure Island* aloud to David. I liked teaching Karen how to ride a bicycle. "Don't let go, Daddy!" Karen called out with nervous laughter as she and I made our way down the street.

I didn't realize that suddenly it would all end. Yes, David went off to college and became a doctor. Karen went off to college and majored in English. And Michael, well, he was the last, the youngest, he was always around, then suddenly *he* was in college and I walked up the stairs one night and found three empty bedrooms.

It has been difficult for me to adjust to what is commonly called "the empty nest." I call it an empty heart. Where are my babies? What happened to the young father who carried the little boy on his back as he counted the stairs? What happened to the man who pushed the little girl on the swing as she called out in glee, "Faster, Daddy! Faster!"

Somehow I think we human beings are not built to say good-bye. We know how to nurture, to love—to build up a home and a family and a place where routine and Scrabble become hints of heaven, and we didn't even know it. And then it is all gone. The games are tucked away in the hall closet, and the children grow up and fall in love, travel, set out for other lives that cast long shadows back to where they once knew the sound of their father's voice.

Letting go is difficult, especially if what we must relinquish is filled with our own inner sense for what is good and comfortable and safe. But we are not creatures locked in time and space. We grow old. The earth revolves around the sun each twenty-four hours no matter how much we wish we could hold back time. But we remember the spinning wheels of a daughter's bicycle, and the laughter of a son's voice when his father made the pirate sound of Long John Silver.

At the end of the Robin Williams film *Hook*, one of the lost boys in Neverland says to Peter Pan just before Peter leaves, "That was a great game."

When I am close to my own end, I hope that I can look up into the eyes of my children and whisper, "That was a great game," for it is in this game of living among those we love where we do, indeed, find greatness. Such greatness cannot be discovered unless we let go of those we love and watch them blossom.

OCTOBER 28

*I cannot think of any need in childhood
as strong as the need for a father's protection.*

—Sigmund Freud

When she was a little girl, my daughter Karen was once a witch for Halloween. Her mother sewed the costume that included a dress with purple moons and a pointed hat that sat on Karen's head in a perfect, witchlike manner.

That October many years ago I held Karen's hand as we walked along the leaf-covered pavement of Woodland Court, a small cul-de-sac at the edge of Morris County, New Jersey—at the edge of paradise.

"Daddy! Look what Mrs. Ryans gave me!" Karen held up like a trophy a small plastic pumpkin filled with chocolate bats and moons that Mrs. Ryans wrapped in orange cellophane especially for her.

I held Karen's hand as we walked from house to house in our small neighborhood, about the size of Harper Lee's town of Maycomb that she created in her iconic novel *To Kill a Mockingbird.*

Karen carried a large, plastic, Halloween pumpkin as her container for her candy, and each time we approached a house, she ran up the stairs saying, "I'm going to ring the doorbell." She and I stood before the closed door of Mr. O'Neal's house as Karen whispered, "I can hear Mrs. O'Neal playing the piano. Should I ring the bell again?" But before I answered, kind, old Mr. O'Neal opened the door, looked down at Karen, smiled, and asked, "And who are you?"

"I'm a witch," Karen said with confidence.

"Do you know that little girl Karen who lives next door?" Mr. O'Neal asked.

"Oh yes, she is making applesauce with her mother," said the witch.

Mr. O'Neal smiled, looked at me, and then asked my daughter, "What do you say?"

"Trick-or-treat," Karen answered as she extended her half-filled plastic pumpkin.

"Happy Halloween," Mr. O'Neal said, as he dropped a small paper bag filled with candy corn into the belly of Karen's happy pumpkin.

"Happy Halloween," Karen called back as she raced down the street.

By the time I caught up with her, she was already running up the driveway to the next house.

After Jody Muller, our neighbor for over thirty years, gave Karen a bar of chocolate, Karen ran to the road, turned to Mrs. Muller, and called out, "Happy Halloween," from under her hat, which allowed her brown hair to dangle along her rosy, October cheeks.

"I got a giant Hershey's Bar," Karen announced. I walked beside her through the dim light of the coming dusk, as we stepped unknowingly into the past.

I walked alongside Karen many times in her life. I escorted her into Sloan-Kettering hospital because the doctors thought she had cancer. (She didn't.) I walked with her to the Fourth of July fireworks over at the high school. She was there, right by my side, as I read to her each night about Clifford the Big Red Dog, or about Eloise and her exploits in Paris.

And then I turned to look at my daughter, and there she was, on my left arm, suddenly walking beside me in her wedding gown.

Autumn is Karen's favorite season: the cornstalks, the harvest moon, the sun illuminating the mottled leaves.

This evening, I looked at one of the photographs from the wedding, Karen leaning against the front railing of the famous little Raritan Inn in Lebanon, New Jersey. There she was with her beautiful smile on her special day, all grown up, married, smart, filled with the hope of a new life.

May all fathers bring their children to such hope. May all fathers see their children grow season to season.

As an anonymous author wrote:

May jack-o'-lanterns burning bright
Of soft and golden hue
Pierce through the future's veil and show
What fate now holds for you.

Happy Halloween, Karen. I will always be by your side.

OCTOBER 29

"I do believe in spooks. I do believe in spooks.
I do! I do! I do! I do believe in spooks.
I do believe in spooks. I do! I do! I do! I do!"

—The Cowardly Lion

Do you remember the wonderful scene in Harper Lee's extraordinary book, *To Kill a Mockingbird*, where Jem and his sister Scout find hidden treasures in the knot of the old tree drooping in the shadows of Boo Radley's house? Do you remember how the children shivered when they realize that scary, mysterious, reclusive Boo Radley himself might, just might, have placed those carved soap sculptures of children and sticks of gum in that tree trunk?

We have, in our tradition of Halloween, the need to be frightened, because of the association this day has with death, witches, ghosts, and fire, but I no longer see evidence that people recreate that genuine feeling of ghoulish scare. We work hard at trying to create authentic fright on Halloween but, in truth, we are disappointed with plastic, moaning machines that echo on the front porch when children step up for candy; fake spiderwebs; Styrofoam tombstones erected beside birdbaths; latex masks that replicate warts and fangs and that, in the end, make the children look like rubber cartoons.

When the three witches in William Shakespeare's *Macbeth* speak, there is an omen-like air of menace and gloom that marks the coming events and that tickles the playgoer's skittish nerves: "Fair is foul, and foul is fair: Hover through the fog and filthy air."

What hovers through the fog of "Hallowed Eve" these days? Candy bars the size of dominoes, curfews, acetate costumes in cardboard and cellophane boxes that parents buy out of convenience and not for the delight of the children. A charcoal beard and a paper eye-patch are far more meaningful to a child than a pirate costume bought at Wal-Mart.

In one of my favorite novels, *A Tale of Two Cities* by Charles Dickens, a curious boy secretly followed his scoundrel of a father, who had crept into a cemetery in the middle of the night. It is there that the boy witnessed his father and two other grave-robbers pulling up a coffin from the ground. The poor boy was so frightened at what he observed that he turned and began to run home. As he looked back, he was convinced that he saw a giant coffin chasing after him. For me, as I read the book for the first time, that image of the haunted coffin was almost as good as those Frankenstein movies with the monster reaching out from the screen and nearly strangling me in the seat on a Saturday afternoon at the theater.

Children aren't placed in a fanciful world of fright and ghouls any longer. They aren't read the tale of Washington Irving's "Headless Horseman," or told about Druids and open fires on the hillside. Children these days are too jaded and would not jump off the couch as they imagined a giant coffin chasing after them.

Today we saturate children with real images of violence, horror, evil, and blood. The nature shows on television gleefully exhibit a lion clawing into its prey at the end of the chase, as the narrator describes the lion's gouging teeth ripping into the neck of the antelope. We display murders in our movies and television programs with explicit gunshot wounds to the head, and exhibits of torture. We splash news headlines of rape and murder between evening comedy shows, and create music that celebrates ugliness, knives, and death.

In the neighborhood where I grew up, there were two old women in their eighties whom we all referred to only as the two little old ladies. I never knew their names. They were twins, wore well-groomed helmets of white hair, and every Sunday walked arm in arm past our house on their way to church. Many times my father offered them a ride home after Sunday Mass, and sometimes the two little old ladies accepted.

I remember sitting in the back seat of the old station wagon as the two women sat to my right. If I said hello, the first lady would turn to me and say, "Hello, Christopher." Then the second old lady would lean forward, look at me, and take her turn: "Hello, Christopher."

They both had hair above their lips, both spoke with puffed cheeks, and both gestured with bony hands. They carried the scent of gardenias and seemed perfectly content to live what I thought was a life from *Alice in Wonderland*. Their house was small, squat, hidden behind a garden of roses and grapevines.

Our family had an affection for the two little old ladies, but there was one thing that stuck with me, one thing that compelled *me* to keep a modest distance from their return affection:

They both wore old-woman, lace-up shoes that were black and had thick heels.

Everything I knew about witches included shoes that looked exactly like the black shoes the two little old ladies wore.

Each time we dropped them off, I watched their shoes as they slowly walked up the path to their little house. I imagined, as they turned and waved goodbye, that they owned a large black cauldron in the backyard, where normal people might build a warm, bubbling Jacuzzi. As I waved out the window of the station wagon, I'd stare at their shoes and shiver a bit, half-expecting the two old women to hover in the fog and filthy air and disappear on their broomsticks.

Let's not do to children what the wonderful children's author of fright R. L. Stine endured when he was young: "When I was a kid my family was really poor and I remember one Halloween I wanted to dress up really scary and my parents came home with a duck costume. I wore that costume for years! I hated it."

Halloween fright is a subtle emotion: far more powerful when triggered by the hint of danger, instead of when forced on the soul with plastic pumpkins and giant, inflatable witches.

OCTOBER 30

"I'm doomed. One little slip like that could cause the Great Pumpkin to pass you by. Oh, Great Pumpkin, where are you?"

—Linus

When Mr. Hinchman, the local carpenter, began construction on the addition to this little house, I asked him if he would install a drop-down, attic stairway so that I could easily access the crawl space. He did, and this morning I reached up once again for the small rope that dangles from the square, hidden cover to the folding steps. I pulled with my left hand and the stairs began to magically appear. I heard the heavy springs expanding as I grabbed the slat of the first step and slowly extended the entire contraption.

The steps wobbled a bit as I began climbing. When I reached the crawl space, I felt like a gopher popping its head out from under the ground. I grabbed another string between my thumb and index finger, and gently pulled until the attic light dimly illuminated the dark space. I smelled dust and stale air.

I like the attic because I like seeing the bare ribs of the house supporting the roof. I like seeing the exposed brick from the furnace chimney. It is like being inside Jonah's whale: bones and ribs inside a cavern of darkness.

I moved my daughter's dollhouse to the right. There was a box marked "David's high school notebooks." Michael's fencing equipment, a crib, teddy bears, Christmas lights, Easter baskets, a train set, luggage, props that accompanied school plays, band competitions, and picnics—all are artifacts of a life well-lived with children and holidays, remnants of happy days.

As I pushed aside little-girl boots, and bins of LEGOs, I found, sitting alone in the corner of the attic, what I had been looking for: the pumpkin.

Many years ago, when the children were small, I bought a two-foot-high, plastic pumpkin with a small electric light in its belly. Every October I brought the pumpkin down from the attic, and propped it up on a small table in the room where I write so that when I plugged it in, the pumpkin lit up, and from the street, anyone who walked or drove by saw the carved, autumn pumpkin in the window.

I remember the sound of the children's voices each autumn as they played in the darkness in the small front yard, and how they chased each other with dried maple leaves, ran after each other in their endless game of flashlight tag, or sat on the front stoop and whispered about Halloween, or witches, or whatever children speak about in the darkness as a glowing pumpkin watches over them from a window.

To me, all of autumn is caught in the crooked smile of that pumpkin. The smiling pumpkin looks out each autumn from the inside part of the house like a beacon guiding the children home, and the center of the season taps the windowpane.

When we look for the center of American literature, we see Walt Whitman's poetry, Herman Melville's *Moby Dick*, and Mark Twain's *Huckleberry Finn*. When we seek the center of American society, we see the Constitution and the Declaration of Independence. When we want to know the essential elements of a marriage, we see the way the man brushes back a strand of hair from his sleeping wife's face, or the way the woman waves when the man is walking up the hill on his way home.

The central moment of a summer holiday might be a certain sunset. Music can be defined by a single robin at dusk. The moon gathers the robe of night around her, and she becomes the center of attention.

What is essential will never abandon us, for it is the core of our existence. Albert Einstein defined the universe with a simple equation. Self is defined by the planet Earth spinning around the burning Sun. Birth becomes the single wail; hunger, a loaf of bread; the desert, a grain of beige sand.

I carried the pumpkin down from the attic and, once again, placed it at the window. I plugged in the light, and the new fall season began.

For me, autumn is defined as a weak light emanating from the belly of a pumpkin, glowing out onto the yard where the children come, one by one, for Halloween or for some other treat, in the chill of cool air, as the pumpkin smiles with his crooked teeth.

When all things are stripped down to their essential elements, we can often find the delight that is boldly there.

OCTOBER 31

Find SEXY Halloween costumes, kids' Halloween costumes,
WORLD-WIDE shipping, adult Halloween costumes,
toddler and baby Halloween costumes.
—Internet sales pitch

I pushed my carriage down the fruit-and-vegetable aisle of the supermarket the other day. I was about to reach for a package of grapes when I saw, sitting on the back ledge of the fruit bin, candy apples individually wrapped in clear, hard plastic. Same wood sticks, as I remembered. Same blood-red coating. Same flat base where the candy had settled before hardening. I wanted a candy apple.

That evening after dinner, after reading the paper, taking out the dog, and settling on the couch to continue reading a biography of Robert Frost, I remembered my candy apple waiting for me on the kitchen counter.

One of the many advantages of being sixty is that you can pretend to be ten years old and really remember what it felt like to be ten. You cannot be ten and pretend to be sixty, for you have no idea what it is like to be sixty. The older we get, the better we are at trying out different ages on a whim. I was a ten-year-old boy reaching up to the kitchen counter for my candy apple.

The first thing I needed to do was simply peel the plastic coating from the treat. The packaging was sealed so tightly that the apple might have survived into the next century. I tried ripping the plastic open. No luck. I tried finding a seam where I could slip in a knife and pry open the hard plastic. Not possible. Finally I cut the apple out of its encasement with scissors.

I carried my late-evening snack to the couch, held the familiar, brown stick in my hand, and bit into the red sugar coating. It was gooey. It was tasteless. It was awful. A candy apple is supposed to have a hard, red, sweet-sugar coating that cracks like an egg when you bite into it. The apple is supposed to be hard, and the apple taste is supposed to mingle with the sugar coating in a way that says Halloween and autumn and ten-year-old children. My apple was soft, limp, and it quickly slipped off the stick. This represents some of the world that we have lost.

Remember those terrific prizes in the Cracker Jack boxes? Tin whistles, metal alligators, frog clickers, and charms....Have you opened a Cracker Jack box recently and seen the sad "prizes" these days? Have you recently bitten into a Devil Dog? Once they were made of delicious chocolate cake, filled with sweet cream, and sold for a nickel. Today a Devil Dog is taste-less, dry, deeply disappointing, and sadly overpriced.

We are living in a world that is trying to make the most amount of profit for the least amount of value, and such a core belief destroys what is charming.

Candy corn no longer has taste. Witches are given electronic cackles and blinking eyes. We buy our children Halloween cos-tumes for $90, and cover our lawns with blow-up balloons of car-toon characters dressed in vampire capes.

I liked being a boy. I liked eating crisp, delicious candy apples. I liked sifting in the fireplace for small bits of coal and smearing it on my face to look like a bum. I liked finding ragged clothes in the basement and running with my sister through the neighborhood, ringing doorbells, hearing Mrs. Costar say what great costumes we had made, as she dropped a full-size Hershey's Bar into our pillow cases. Do you see the candy we give to chil-dren these days? Little nothings smaller than a credit card.

How is it that we work so hard at being adults—buying big cars, big houses, important name brands—and we find it so dif-ficult to retain our childlike qualities?

The writer and philosopher Henry David Thoreau wrote in *Walden*, his most famous book, "I would rather sit on a pumpkin and have it all to myself, than to be crowded on a velvet cushion."

Today we adults seem to want that cushion, that velvet, that fancy Halloween decoration, the greatest return for our dol-lar, the hype in preparation for the Christmas boom.

Don't we remember that kids like to make their own cos-tumes? Kids like candy corn that sticks to their teeth and tastes like real sugar. Kids like hard candy apples that crackle. They like to imagine that they see a witch flying past the full moon out their windows. Kids like to carve pumpkins and stick their hands into the goo and pull out the seeds.

Halloween has lost much of its charm because of what we adults have done. Kids like the goo.

NOVEMBER 15

The greatest gift is a portion of yourself.

—Ralph Waldo Emerson

Each November for the past eight years, I would knock on the door of my neighbor's house and ask him if I could borrow his twenty-four-foot aluminum extension ladder so that I could clean out the autumn leaves from my gutters.

Each November, Barry would pull on his plaid coat and his work gloves, and escort me out back behind his house, where he kept the ladder under the crawl space. The two of us would stoop down and make our way through old cobwebs, reshuffle a Big Wheel bike, drag a hose out of the way.

"Are you going to your folks' home for Thanksgiving this year?" I'd ask.

"Same as last year," he'd answer.

Barry would grab one end of the ladder and I'd grab the other end.

He and his wife Patty came to the baptisms of my children, and handed down the pants, shirts, and boots their children outgrew. Each Christmas, Patty sent over the best homemade gingerbread men I have ever eaten.

"Let me help you get this thing over," Barry would say, as I jumped over the thin wire fence that separated our yards. The ladder wasn't really heavy. We just enjoyed playing out our roles in the neighborhood.

"I really should buy one of these things."

"Why bother? You can use it anytime."

Barry and I met for lunch once at his company dining room, which overlooked Manhattan. His treat. My family and I sat in his house for five or six hours while the oil company came to repair our stalled furnace one February night.

"The pulley system sticks a bit. You might want to grab hold of the rung as you extend the ladder."

"I'll get it back in a few hours."

"No hurry. If I'm not home, just leave it on the other side of the fence," Barry would say with a quick wave as he returned to his house.

Each November.

This past spring, when the "For Sale" sign appeared on Barry's front lawn, it was difficult for me to accept that his company was really leaving New York City for Dallas.

As people began to arrive with the Realtors—even when the moving van stood before Barry's house—I still didn't react as I should have. When events play themselves out to an inevitable end, I tend to stand back and observe.

On the day he and his family left, I should have embraced Barry. I simply shook his hand and said good-bye. As he drove down the street, I should have waved and waved and waved, but I didn't.

In the early evening, as I was pulling my son's tricycle in for the day, I found, leaning against the side of my garage, the twenty-four-foot aluminum extension ladder.

THANKSGIVING

We can only be said to be alive in those moments
when our hearts are conscious of our treasures.

—Thornton Wilder

While investigating a small leak in the roof, I found my son's
two-foot sailboat leaning on its side deep inside the attic. The
hull, made of plastic, is red. The deck is blue. The sails are white.
When I bought the boat twenty years ago, I thought it would be
a nice idea to imitate the pleasure of sailing little ships in the
fountains of Paris that I had seen when I was a young man. I
remember little French boys in shorts running from one side of
the fountain to the other. They were given long poles to guide
their sailboats or turn them around. There was something old-
world and postcard charming about the boys and their boats, so
I bought my son a sailboat, gave him a long stick, and drove him
to our local park.

The pond was about the size of a basketball court filled
with sticks and mud. As my son launched the boat into the
water, it immediately hooked itself to a rotting maple branch. He
shrugged his shoulder and said, "Let's go home."

I carried the boat back to the house, and twenty years later
I found it in the attic. I picked it up, held it in my hand, felt the
small sails, and moments later I was standing beside the pond at
the park. The water is clear now. A fountain of water gushes
wonderfully from the center. The pond is free of sticks, leaves,
and mud. I leaned over and placed the small boat into the water,
and, with a small stick that I found, I pushed the boat out from

the shore. A movement of air filled the sails, and the boat leaned to the side, and began to glide effortlessly across the pond.

Life is sometimes just a stale, muddy pond with rotting sticks and leaves, and it is also at times a glorious lake filled with clear water and gushing fountains. The secret is hidden in what we build to cross that water.

We human beings are given the gift of intellect to overcome physical obstacles in our lives. We are given a soul to overcome challenges to the spirit of who we are. When I found that small boat in the attic, I felt a surge of thanksgiving for the existence of my three children. They have been at the center of my life for the past twenty-five years. They are what have kept Roe and me afloat. My inner life is sometimes clouded, filled with loneliness or rough seas, but then my daughter calls, or my son appears at the door, or my eldest son sends a letter, and I am reminded, once again, what has kept my sails bound tightly to the mast of my life.

Each year we celebrate Thanksgiving, a celebration of the harvest and the memory that early settlers survived another winter.

We have, in our hearts, a notion of paradise. For me, in part, paradise has a wonderful, wide fountain that looks just like the one in Paris and I am wearing little shorts and am guiding my blue-and-red boat from one side of the water to the next. For me, paradise includes my three children writing me letters and surprising me at the front door.

The November holiday is a time to give thanks that we have an intellect to imagine the truth of paradise, and a time to give thanks that we have a soul to guide us along the way. Thanksgiving is a time to stand beside our husbands and wives, our children, our mothers and father, our aunts and uncles, our neighbors and friends, and be grateful for the bounty of what it means to be a family.

NOVEMBER 22

A man may die, nations may rise and fall, but an idea lives on.
—John F. Kennedy

Earthquakes. Fires. War. Mud slides. Suicide bombings. Hurricanes.

Some people predict that this is the end of the world. For me, the end of the world arrived at the edge of my life on November 22, 1963, when I heard the principal whisper in the ear of my seventh-grade spelling teacher, "The president was shot."

Up until that Friday afternoon almost fifty years ago, I was a boy who believed in immortality, couldn't wait for Christmas, walked home each day after school over the train tracks, and looked forward to eating my mother's apple pie and watching *Superman* on the television.

There were three distinct places in my world when I was a child: the celery farm, the public swimming pool, and the train tracks.

Behind the house where I grew up in Allendale, New Jersey, there is what was always called, when I was a child, the celery farm. It was a place with wide canals and banks of reeds and soft marshes that cushioned duck nests in the spring and children lacing their ice skates in the winter.

My brothers and sisters and I spent many days under the hot summer sun hunting for snapping turtles in the celery farm. "There's one!" And we'd stop and watch the turtle's large head protruding up through the water, or we'd watch the entire turtle pass under us at the small bridge at the southern tip of the swamp.

I learned how to ice-skate on the frozen ditches. We played

hockey and ice tag, brought an old bedsheet and held it tightly between us as we sailed down the long canals. I felt brave and confident as my sister and I skated back and forth through the reeds as the blades of our skates click-clacked against the frozen water. I liked kneeling down and, with my gloved hand, pushing away the frost and snow to look eye to eye at the giant goldfish that swam under the haze of the thick ice.

In the summer, my sister and I swam at the Allendale public pool: a wide, blue, concrete pool that had a raft in the middle, trees on either side, and a small road where the white ice-cream truck arrived each day in the late morning.

Sometimes, on a slow Sunday afternoon, I pulled my red bicycle out of the garage and zoomed down Franklin Turnpike. I often bought a Ring Ding, then rode my bike to the Allendale train depot, sat on the roof of the underpass, and waited for the next train.

As I ate my chocolate-covered cake, sucking out the whipped cream, soon enough the train appeared around the bend. When the great engine approached, I stood up and waved at the engineer. He waved back every time with his blue-striped engineer gloves. We were in control of the universe, the engineer and I.

On that Friday afternoon of November 22, the day President Kennedy was murdered, the principal closed the school early, and I walked home past the blue swimming pool, over the train tracks, past the celery farm, and when I entered the house, I found my mother and father standing in the kitchen. My father was crying. I had never seen my father cry.

We are safe as long as the fathers are strong, I thought when I was boy, and there was my father, so shaken in the kitchen. And there, a few days later, was John Kennedy, Jr., saluting his father's coffin as it was carried along the black avenue.

I stopped going to the train station and waving to the engineer. I found out that George Reeves, the actor who played

Superman, committed suicide. The town filled in the swimming pool. I went to the senior prom with a girl whose father was killed in Vietnam.

Earthquakes. Fires. War. Mud slides. Suicide bombings. Hurricanes. My world as a boy ended.

Some years ago, the little town of Allendale decided that the celery farm ought to become a public wildlife preserve. It is a place, now, for swans, mallards, herons, fox, deer, cormorants. You can still watch the snapping turtles swim under the bridge in the hot summers, and see the goldfish under the ice in winter.

In a speech at American University in Washington, DC, on June 10, 1963, President Kennedy said, "For in the final analysis, our most basic common link is that we all inhabit this small planet, we all breathe the same air, we all cherish our children's futures, and we are all mortal."

November 22, 1963, was a remarkably sad day in the history of our nation, but I will follow John Kennedy's sentiments. I will recognize the glory of our small planet in the sound of the red-winged blackbirds balancing on the brown reeds in the celery farm, hold my children's hands as we look for snapping turtles, and accept that our time is short together, as we celebrate what is brave, beautiful, and good to protect now and at the last moment of this spinning, confusing world.

DECEMBER 1

If my doctor told me I had only six minutes to live,
I wouldn't brood. I'd type a little faster.

—Isaac Asimov

Each day I am driven to my desk to write. People like to speculate about writer's block, or about lost talent, or about the habits of doing the same thing that can lead to creation.

I never have writer's block, and I believe that writers improve their craft the more they read and write. The more we read, the more different sorts of sentence patterns we assimilate, the more vocabulary words we acquire, the more emotional swords strike into our hearts. I have discovered, for my own writing, that all this is true, but there is something more.

I began to write when I was twenty-three because I was lonely, and I filled my longing with poetry and the muse. The more I wrote, the greater my purpose was to write. I wanted to share my vision of happiness with people. I wanted to entertain.

Fred Rogers, the man many of us knew from *Mister Rogers' Neighborhood*, asked me one day, while we were visiting Henri Nouwen in Toronto, Canada: "Do you ever feel the presence of the Holy Spirit inside of you when you write?"

No one had ever asked me to make a connection between creativity and God. While I suspected there was a connection, I avoided the notion. Actually, I feared the connection for I did not want to be considered a "religious" writer, and I did not want to admit that I felt there was a greater power beyond my own talents that infused creativity into my mind and pen. Artists like doing it alone, plus I knew, I just knew, that for me there is the reality of a true calling to a vocation.

We come to our life's work along mysterious paths. I pretended that I became a writer because both my mother and father wrote, because I was lonely and needed a diversion, because I was arrogant and I could do it.

When I write, I feel as if I enter a world beyond the ordinary wind blowing and the cars passing before my window.

When a child jumps into the lake water in summer, he yells with glee. When a man and woman exchange marriage vows, they sense a grace and spiritual upheaval that they identify as love. This is good. When we bake bread, cut the lawn, visit a museum—we find again and again a sense of it all, a feeling that we cannot identify, but know is there just the same.

That feeling is what I feel when I complete an essay, or when I am engaged in the writing of a poem. For me, writing is exchanging vows with those I love: my readers. For me, when I write, I feel as if I am jumping in the cool lake while holding my father's hand as we both yell together. Writing poetry is just as luxurious as moving from painting to painting in the great museums, and feeling what we feel when we glimpse beauty.

Our mortal lives contain bits of time and offer us glimpses of paradise, and, if we recognize the beauty, we step away with a sense of a universal love and promise that there is hope and salvation.

"A writer tries to help people recognize beauty," I explained to Fred, and he said, "That is good."

DECEMBER 4

Help your brother's boat across, and your own will reach the shore.
                                        —Hindu proverb

My older brother Oliver was a "vegetable" for thirty-two years. The best guess is that he endured severe brain damage before he was born. He was blind. He had no intellect. He could not chew, talk, or respond.

For thirty-two years, Oliver lay on his back in his bed. My father shaved his beard. My mother fed him breakfast and lunch. My brothers and sisters and I took turns feeding him dinner.

Often my sister and I were the "lifters" when it was time to bathe Oliver. I remember how it was: My mother prepared the bath towels and the water in the tub. My father directed my sister and me. Anne climbed onto the bed, sat on the headboard, and gently slipped her hands under Oliver's armpits. I stood at the end of the bed and with my arms cradled Oliver's legs. Then my father reached under Oliver's back, and the three of us pulled my brother up out of the bed and slowly carried him through the room.

I remember my mother calling out from the bathroom: "Don't bump his elbows against the doorsill." When my father, sister, and I reached the door, I remember how nervous I was not to knock Oliver's elbows into the doorsill.

Oliver was heavy. We carried him down the long hallway. His skin was smooth. He breathed calmly as we stepped into the bathroom.

"Anne, walk carefully around now to the back of the tub," my mother said, as my sister slowly walked through the little room, laboriously bending as she firmly held Oliver.

"Chrissy, now swing his legs along to the side of the tub."

"Mom. We've done this a hundred times."

My mother smiled. "Okay, Anne, lift him over the edge, and, Chrissy, you do the same thing, but place his legs gently into the water first."

I lifted Oliver over the edge of the white tub and placed his legs into the warm water. Each time I see marine biologists on television slip rescued dolphins back into the blue ocean, I think of Oliver's white, little legs slowly submerging into the bath water.

"Anne, now lower his shoulders and head."

Oliver sank into the tub. His head rested against a towel my father held. And then my sister and I watched as my mother bathed him. She lathered a blue washcloth with pink soap and sponged his body, and, as she bathed him, she spoke, sometimes saying to us, "Oliver is grateful that you helped him today," or she might sing a French lullaby as she washed his hair. My father would cup his hands around Oliver's forehead so that the shampoo would not seep into my brother's brown eyes.

Oliver was in a perpetual comatose state, unaware of his surroundings, incapable of any intellectual or emotional function that would be considered normal, except for one thing: he laughed. Sometimes when my family and I were asleep, we would all be awoken in the middle of the night by this deep, husky laughter. Oliver would laugh and laugh, and that is all.

Oliver died in my mother's arms of pneumonia. As he pulled in his last breath and exhaled into silence, my mother whispered, "Good-bye, my angel." After feeding him, bathing him, and loving him for thirty-two years: "Good-bye, my angel."

The quality of a person's life is not determined by the present state of comfort and worthiness. The quality of a person's life is determined by the cumulative results of that life.

I think back to those days when a boy and a girl carried their brother down a long, dark hall. I think back to a father holding a towel, to a mother bathing her son and singing,

> "Frère Jacques, frère Jacques,
> Dormez-vous? Dormez-vous?
> Sonnez les matines! Sonnez les matines!
> Ding, dang, dong! Ding, dang, dong!"

Are you sleeping, my brother Oliver? Are you sleeping?
I guess you could call him a vegetable.
Are you sleeping?
I called him Oliver, my brother.
Morning bells are ringing. Morning bells are ringing.
You would have liked him.

Ding, dang, dong!
We have the power to sit and nurture all that grows
      around us.
Ding, dang, dong!

DECEMBER 19

I stopped believing in Santa Claus when I was six.
Mother took me to see him in a department store
and he asked for my autograph.

—Shirley Temple

Many famous people were born in New Jersey: Frank Sinatra, Aaron Burr, William Carlos Williams, Norman Schwarzkopf, Derek Jeter. But I know a secret about New Jersey that only a few people know, and my telling you this secret will be just as startling as telling you that Clark Kent is really Superman.

I know where Santa Claus lives, and I know his secret identity. I've had my suspicions for the past thirty years, and now I believe I have enough evidence to tell you that Santa Claus lives in Pompton Plains, New Jersey.

When Roe and I married in 1977, we moved into our little house here in Pompton Plains, where we still live. We've raised three children, two cats, a dog, some mice, and a few goldfish. I have done everything possible to make sure this house stayed warm, cool, bug-free, painted, nailed, windowed, screened, wired, and safe. And each time I needed nails, rake, paint, shovels, washers, lightbulbs, seeds—no matter what I needed for the house—I'd drive to Jones Hardware Store, which sits at the corner of the Newark-Pompton Turnpike and Jackson Avenue. You can't miss it. It's slate blue with red shutters, and has a nice overhang roof and a chimney. It looks like a building right out of George Bailey's Bedford Falls. I can nearly hear Jimmy Stewart saying, "Why, ah, why it's right there, ah, next to the Building and Loan."

For thirty years I have walked into Jones Hardware Store, and each time Rob—a tall, burly man with glasses, a smile, a booming laugh, and a gentle kindness—each time Rob has welcomed me with a weather report, a joke, and an encouraging word. And no matter what I ask for, he always has it. If an item is not displayed in the store, Rob will walk "down the basement" and, within minutes, reemerge with what I requested.

During the past thirty years, I have never been "down the basement" of the hardware store. There are only two explanations concerning its existence: either the basement to the hardware store is the size of the state of Texas, or it is magical. I just cannot believe that Rob could store all that he apparently has in the basement without having some sort of access to a space that is either an underground engineering feat or....Well, I'm jumping ahead of myself here.

One summer, I was looking for grass seed. When I stepped into the store, the place was empty. I called out. No one answered. I called out again, and there came this husky laughter from outside. "I'm in the barn, Chris." There was Rob, painting Santa Claus.

Each Christmas season, Rob climbs onto the roof of the hardware store and ties a large wood cutout of Santa to the chimney. The cutout sits in a sleigh behind a fancy, happy reindeer.

I looked at Rob in his red shirt and black boots.

"I'm just touching up this Christmas decoration for next season," he said.

I looked at Rob again, and then at the wood replica.

Hmmm.

When our children were small, Roe and I signed up for the town fire department to bring Santa to our house. During a cold December evening, the neighborhood suddenly lit up with red lights. The children ran to the window and watched as Santa Claus stepped off the fire truck and began walking to the front of the house.

"Ho! Ho! Ho!" Santa bellowed as he stepped in. The children clapped as Santa handed them bits of candy. Roe smiled. I looked at Santa Claus, and he looked at me, and he said, with warmth and goodness, "Merry Christmas, Chris." I almost said "Merry Christmas, Rob," but I didn't want to give away his secret identity.

I cannot say that my life for the past thirty years has been easy. Life never is. Deaths, disappointments, bills, illnesses, pangs of loneliness, children rushed to the hospital. Often, when I stepped into the hardware store for drain cleaner or a bag of nails, Rob asked about me, or remembered that my father was ill. He loaned me fertilizer spreaders and deck-stain sprayers, and he often "forgot" to charge me for an item.

Rob doesn't know the countless times his humor and encouraging words made the greatest difference at that particular moment in my life. For many years, I'd say that Rob was like Bert the cop in *It's a Wonderful Life*, or Ernie the cabdriver. He reminded me of the Ghost of Christmas Present in Charles Dickens' *A Christmas Carol*: sure of himself, larger than life, full of merriment and wise warnings.

Rob loves the winter, and he talks about deer with great enthusiasm. I do not know a kinder man. I do not know how he can have so much stored in the basement. I do not know how he created a store lifted right out of a Norman Rockwell painting. There is only one explanation: Rob Jones *is* Santa Claus.

When word speared throughout England that Charles

Dickens died, it is famously known that a little girl called out in a plaintive cry, "Mr. Dickens dead? Then will Father Christmas die too?"

No, child, he is alive and well, and he sits behind the counter of his hardware store in Pompton Plains, New Jersey. Of course, a hardware store. A great cover. He orders all he needs: tools, wheels, wire, and wood to make all those toys deep down inside that magic basement.

Derek Jeter was born in Pompton Plains, but Santa Claus lives here.

Winter

I prefer winter and fall, when you feel the bone structure
of the landscape—the loneliness of it, the dead feeling of winter.
Something waits beneath it, the whole story doesn't show.

—Andrew Wyeth

DECEMBER 20

But it is a cold, lifeless business when you go to the shops
to buy something, which does not represent your life and talent,
but a goldsmith's.

—Ralph Waldo Emerson

I am sixty years old, and I am pushing brown, dried cloves into the tight skin of an orange.

When I was eight, I asked my mother what she wanted for Christmas, and she said, "A closet freshener."

"What's a closet freshener?" I asked.

My mother led me into the yellow kitchen with the high, tin ceiling, reached into a straw basket for an orange, and returned from the pantry with a bottle of cloves. "Now, poke the cloves into the orange until the orange is completely covered," she said, as she demonstrated how to insert the first clove. "Make rows up and down as you turn the orange."

On the morning of December 25, 1959, my mother opened a white box and found a dried orange covered in a neat grid of hard, fragrant cloves. She insisted that it was the best gift she received that Christmas, and so for the past fifty-two years since then I have made for my mother an orange-and-clove pomander.

I would like to call this small event a tradition, but it goes deeper than that. It is a moment etched into my own fragile heart. I am just a player, much like children in a snow globe: part of the scenery whenever someone shakes the little glass ball.

All happiness comes to us in seemingly insignificant ways. A few months after each of our three children was born, Roe sewed a Christmas stocking and lined it with the new child's receiving blanket from the hospital. Robbie Jones, the proprietor of the local hardware store, sits on top of the town's fire engine each December and plays Santa Clause. I still run to the window and watch the flashing red lights and Santa's white gloves waving and waving in the darkness.

When I was nine years old, my father spent every free moment during the months of November and early December sawing, hammering, and sanding in the basement. I was forbidden to open the door to his workshop during those weeks of secret work. That Christmas I received a wooden fort for my tin soldiers. It was sand yellow, and had a moat painted in blue, a drawbridge that worked, and turrets! It still, to this day, remains one of the best Christmas gifts that I have ever received.

We are a people in fast pursuit of happiness. We shuttle back and forth between our jobs and homes. We build bigger cars, faster jets, taller buildings. We change homes every seven years. Little seems to stay in place.

My mother and father moved to this country in 1948, and bought a house just beyond a celery farm in a small town west of New York City. It is a three-story place with cedar shingles. The concrete steps still have the same cracks as then. The front door opens wide into the foyer, where the aroma of bread or soup or turkey floats in the air. To the right is where the Christmas tree is set up each December, right in the middle of the living room. My parents have lived in this house for the past sixty-three years.

Oh, here's my mother. She is a writer, one of the smartest people I know, and she makes terrific pea soup. And this is my father. He writes too and he is the smartest person I know. He was a book editor and a college professor. And here is where I sat and watched President Kennedy's funeral on the television. I can take you upstairs and show you my bedroom. It still has posters of the Beatles tacked on the wall. My mother is eighty-nine years old. My father is ninety-nine years old. Norman Rockwell might just as well have painted this house as any other.

Last year it snowed on Christmas day. When Roe and I returned to our house, after spending my fifty-ninth Christmas in the house of my mother and father, I turned on the lights and let the dog out the back door. As I stood on the deck, I noticed, in the new snow, deer tracks. I had never seen a deer in the yard, not even deer tracks, but there they were. If I told you that I also saw the tracks of a sleigh, you would probably not believe me, so I won't.

But I can tell you this. This year I will be spending my six-tieth Christmas in the same house where I have spent all the Christmas days of my life, and my mother is getting a dried orange covered in cloves.

We think that we are in pursuit of happiness when, in real-ity, it has already been found a long time ago when the pea soup was hot and the tin soldiers successfully protected the Christmas fort once again.

DECEMBER 21

And death shall have no dominion...

—Dylan Thomas

My mother called this morning to tell me that my father had another episode. "He was walking down the stairs to the living room when he felt disoriented, dizzy, weak. He had to sit on the stairs." She assured me that I did not have to stop by. "He took his medication. The doctor said it was another ministroke. He is perfectly fine now."

I hate death. I love the sound of the mockingbird. I love the taste of tomato soup. I love the sound of the voices of my children, the curve of Roe's back. I like riding a bicycle in spring. I laugh at Laurel and Hardy in the desert.

When I was a boy and it snowed, I pulled on my black boots with the metal clips, wrapped a wool scarf around my neck, dipped my arms into the sleeves of my gray coat, pulled on a stocking hat, and rushed out to the woods in the back, and pretended that I lived in an ice castle.

I loved following the tracks of a rabbit in the snow, sucking on an icicle, skating with my sisters and brothers.

I watched the birth of my three children, walked along a Roman road in Belgium with Roe, hung Christmas wreaths on the front windows thirty-four times.

I wrote a poem this past winter about some growing, dying thing. The poem is about this house where I live, and about the routines of our lives that, if we look closely, we do cherish, after all.

"I do not know any other thing," the first lines states. I do not know any other thing but my life and routines. We all live an examined life in one way or another. We need to ask ourselves why and where to? All I know is the route I take each day from the house to my job. We wake. We go to work. We toil and return in the evening. There is no other pattern in human existence. We tend to a growing place and do what has never been done beyond our own acreage.

I love marzipan, my mother's laughter, black-eyed Susans, chocolate ice cream, Texas.

We are born to a century. In the poem, I created the fiction that I was born on a farm and learned the skills of the scythe and plow handed down to me from my father. We all learn from our fathers. If they are there beside us or if they abandon us, the lesson is still there: fathers either stand beside their sons or leave them to survive on their own. There is no third choice. I always hoped that I was a worthy student of my father's critical eye.

We are bred by words as human beings. Whales communicate with clicks and whistles. We learn from the words of our elders. We watch what they do with their hands.

Parents smoke, their children will smoke. Parents love, and children will love. Parents read, and children will read.

The lesson adults need to pass along to children is the sweet knowledge that is sucked from a stem of grass.

Often, when I am tired and lonely, I dream that I could have been a world traveler, a famous statesman, an admired salesman from coast to coast, but then I hear the voice of my father coming home each night when I was a child, the voice of stability announcing, "I'm home."

I love the streetlight outside my window, the sound of crickets in mid-August, Mallowmars, *The Great Gatsby*, William Carlos Williams, *Mister Rogers' Neighborhood*, Dylan Thomas, Vermont, Memling, the Madawaska River in Ontario, Canada.

Edmund Gwenn, the English actor who played Santa Claus in the famous little film *The Miracle on 34th Street*, said on his death bed: "Dying is easy. Comedy is difficult."

Of course, I do not make light of the fact that life is difficult. I have known the sorrow of my ill brother, the loss of love, the grief of watching my own children suffer, the roar of genocide, the threat of nuclear weapons, the rage of hurricanes and giant waves. Yes, we can hang our heads and repent, "Lord have mercy." But there is a great mystery in our living. Some survive for a bit of time, and some do not. When I was young, I agreed with the writer William Saroyan. His last words were, "Everybody has got to die, but I have always believed an exception would be made in my case. Now what?"

In the accumulation of days, more and more we are asked, "Now what?" We move forward from being children at play in the fields of the Lord, to being old men and women, brushing back what is left behind us with a wave that is either dismissive or victorious, and then there is the dying. We are all, as survivors, obliged to answer that question, "What next?"

In my poem I wrote, "There is no better place to die than in the circle from house to land and so back again where telling is, in the near end, a choice to be a part of some growing, dying thing." There is no better place to live than in the honorable routines of our lives. There is no better choice to make than to be a part of some growing, dying thing.

Do you realize that a flower in spring is already in a cycle of death? So pick the flowers and spread their petals on the graves of those we love. Memorize the color of the rose.

We celebrate Christmas in late December because of the early jubilation surrounding the winter solstice. December 21 is the shortest day of the year, and then the next day begins the new cycle, and the days begin to extend the light once again, so we come to honor Christmas as the season of light.

"And death shall have no dominion," Dylan Thomas wrote, no supreme authority over life, bones, stars, gulls, waves, rain, daisies. Death shall have no power over some growing, dying thing that we, in our fear and loneliness, have to define.

Some Growing, Dying Thing

I do not know any other thing
But the circle from the house to the land,
A growing place and doing that I have
Never seen beyond my own acreage.

We are born to a century,
And I to a scythe and plow.
My father didn't have a degree

But knew the sample of each
Part of ground and was the
Scholar and I his worthy student.

We are bred by words and
Gestures of the hand,
A telling of the labor that
Brings a sweet knowledge
Sucked from a stem of grass.

Each time I think that perhaps
I've missed a chance at some
Other train or stranger,
Whenever I hear the great wheels
On the tracks that run a straight
Line from west to east,
Whenever a salesman comes to
My door with brown shoes
And a sample case,
I listen for the steel,
Run my hands along the
Pots and silk shirts,
Admit a usefulness
For trains and ties,
And when there is just about
A sale, or a choice to
Buy a ticket for some other
Leap across the line,
I hear my father's voice
With a measured clod of earth
In his hands.

There is no better place to die
Than in the circle from house to land
And so back again where telling
Is, in the near end, a choice to
Be a part of some growing, dying thing.

DECEMBER 22

Up on the housetop, click, click, click…

—song by Jane Whitman

At four o'clock in the morning I woke up to a loud *thud* in the attic. I said to my wife, "I'll get a Havahart trap tomorrow and catch that squirrel." She was asleep, of course, and I decided that the noise I heard was part of a dream, until there was another distinctive thud, like the sound of an elbow hitting the attic floor. Our cat jumped off our bed and leaped up on the dresser searching for the mouse that he probably imagined in his mind.

"It's Santa Claus," I said aloud as a joke, hoping Roe was awake. She wasn't. Then I began to be a boy again and imagined the noise was Marley's ghost from the book I am currently reading: Charles Dickens' *A Christmas Carol.*

"Old Marley probably rattling his chains in the attic next to the summer fans," I thought to myself. It made perfect sense to me that a character from a nineteenth-century British novel would be rolling around in my attic. I had a dream once that William Shakespeare asked for my autograph.

When I was fully awake, I was convinced that a squirrel invited a friend and they were having an acorn-rolling competition, and then I looked out the window. It had snowed during the night, the first New Jersey snow, unexpected and beautiful. Then I realized that the snow was falling in heavy chunks from the branches that loomed over our house and landing with a thud on the roof. No ghost. No squirrel. No Santa Claus. Just clumps of snow.

The next evening, while I was reading the Dickens' novel after a long day at work, red flashing lights began to swirl around the room. I looked out the window across the snow-covered ground and there, entering my neighbor's house, the one with the two small children, was Santa Claus, specially delivered to the neighborhood on the town's fire truck.

"You know," I said to the cat as it looked at me from his seat on the couch, "I used to believe in Santa Claus." The cat blinked, placed his head on his outstretched paws, and closed his eyes.

The famous child star Shirley Temple said, "I stopped believing in Santa Claus when I was six. Mother took me to see him in a department store and he asked me for my autograph."

When the fire engine pulled away from my neighbor's house, I ran through the living room to get a better view, hoping to see Santa Claus sitting in the truck. I made it to the front window just as the flashing lights illuminated the façade of the house. I stood at my window and waved. Santa saw me and waved back. I was eight years old all over again.

When I returned to the couch and my book, the cat hopped onto my lap and curled up like a doughnut. I wanted to ask him if *he* believed in Santa Claus, but I worried that he might actually raise his head and say yes in a perfect British accent.

Our three children are grown and gone. Our dog is dead. Roe is comfortably sleeping upstairs. I am reading the last pages of *A Christmas Carol*. "I will honor Christmas in my heart, and try to keep it all the year," said the reformed Scrooge. "I will live in the Past, the Present, and the Future."

For Christmas this year, I'd like to ask for a collection of tin soldiers, but better things are expected of me, so I won't.

"Meow."

DECEMBER 23

"Isn't there anyone who knows what Christmas is all about?"
—Charlie Brown

The attack was imminent. The horizon was outlined with the enemy on horses. Each soldier held a long spear in his right hand. There was a distant drumming, a fragile rhythm to imitate the beating heart. I was just a boy and knew that the safest place against my impending death was to hide on the roof of the chicken coop, and that is where I slept last night in my dream, my cheek against the rough shingles, my legs curled up against my chest. Then my father appeared, suddenly laying beside me with soothing words: "Do not be afraid."

When I woke up this morning, the last part of the dream that I remembered was a Hun, or a Nazi, someone dressed in black and silver rushing toward me with a lance, topped with a silver, sharp point. The villain was just about to crash through my bedroom window for the kill when my father, like Merlin, waved his right hand over me and the dream evaporated into this December morning.

My father was born two months before the Titanic sank. He has been a quiet, reserved man all of his life. He built sailboats as a hobby when he was young, was one of the glider pilots in the Belgian army, endured the Nazi occupation, became a lawyer, married, emigrated to the United States in 1948, translated books from the Greek and Latin, built a weaving loom, taught French and philosophy in various colleges, joined a publishing firm, drove me to the New York World's Fair in 1963, built me a wooden castle for Christmas, and has been home for all of my sixty years of life. Home, that place, as Robert Frost wrote, "where, when you have to go there, they have to take you in."

I am disturbed the most this Christmas season, beyond all other Christmas seasons, about the blatant commercialism: stores advertising sweatshirts and slippers with upbeat jingles that were once holy Christmas hymns that my father and I sang in church.

In the newspapers, children are being targeted to desire combat video games. More than ever, corporations promote the idea that there is a direct relationship between how much you love someone and how much money you spend on that person, whether it is to purchase a diamond ring or a luxury automobile. Deliver the joy...Buy the perfect gift...Get a free picture with Santa with $100 proof of purchase. Beneath the false gaiety is the ill will and despair of a Pottersville.

Every Wednesday my father returned home from work with a large, cardboard box. He received, as part of his salary, a freshly butchered chicken, two dozen eggs, a rump roast, and fresh vegetables. My father made great pancakes. He cut out the best paper planes, which we flew at birthday parties and spring evenings out on the back lawn: children tossing up little white planes, which spun around the yard like angels.

I heard my father read aloud stories by P. G. Wodehouse, watched him at his desk as he typed his manuscripts, listened with hope that the sound I heard outside was his car tires spinning down the driveway at the end of the day. Daddy was home.

We save up money during the year in our Christmas clubs so that we have enough cash to buy gifts no one really wants or needs. Each night the news reports the national sales figures, comparing this Christmas buying season to last year's. We rush from store to store in our attempts to please those we love with the perfect gift.

Oana, my daughter-in-law, said a few weeks ago that Thanksgiving is her favorite holiday. There is no pressure, no gifts, just the family gathering over a meal and expressing gratitude to God for our lives, for our health, for our families.

To me, Santa Claus is Atticus Finch being there for his children Jem and Scott as they endure the loss of their mother. To me, always, the idea of giving gifts at Christmas was to replicate the three kings bearing gold, frankincense, and myrrh to the Christ child.

The new, garish star at the top of the Christmas tree in Rockefeller Center in New York doesn't come close to the shooting stars my father pointed out to me when I was a boy, just before he and I entered the cabin during our July Canadian vacation.

This afternoon I know where my father will be: in his chair beside the fireplace reading the history of China, or up on the rooftop where reindeer pause. Out of the sleigh jumps good old Santa Claus, my father, leaning over me, whispering in my dreams, "Do not be afraid, Christopher." That is the Christmas message sent down to us through the ages from good Saint Nick.

DECEMBER 24

Santa Claus, also known as Saint Nicholas, Father Christmas, Kris Kringle, or simply "Santa," is a historical, legendary, and mythical figure in folklore who, in Western cultures, is described as bringing gifts on Christmas Eve or Christmas Day, or on his feast day, December 6.

—Wikipedia

I once had the idea that Santa Claus was Mr. Lukaszewski, the wonderful old man who lived beyond our back woods in a small house that sat like a mushroom alongside the tall reeds of the local swamp. He spoke little English, raised chickens, and let my sister and me gather from the henhouse the six eggs my mother ordered each week. I liked to hold a new, warm egg in my hand and place it against my cheek.

Mr. Lukaszewski always had a supply of used egg cartons made of thick, gray paper. I liked watching him take the eggs from my sister and me one by one and slowly place each egg in each cupped space. They looked like six little knees in a gray box.

As I counted out the coins and placed them in Mr. Lukaszewski's hand, he often spoke kind words in Polish, kind I knew because he smiled, and then he always said thank-you: "*Dzieki.*"

"I bet he's Santa Claus," I said to my sister once as we made our way back home through the thick woods, pushing our way through an early December snow.

"Nah," she said. "Santa Claus is just Mom buying presents and wrapping them up." I emerged from the woods a bit wiser, I suppose, but also a bit suspicious that my sister was wrong.

That night, while the rest of the family was watching television, I crept to the closet, pulled my coat from a hook, grabbed my wool hat, and dipped my feet into my black, rubber boots—the ones with the black clips. Then I slipped out the back door, down the wooden stairs, and out into the frozen night.

I quickly ran into the woods and began to follow the footprints that my sister and I had made in the snow earlier that day. The moon was bright. The bare trees cast their long, dark shadows against the pale, blue-night snow. I was going to see if old Mr. Lukaszewski was really Santa Claus.

In the middle of the woods, I found fresh icicles dangling from the underside of a low tree branch. I broke off one of the bits of ice and sucked it, pretending it was sugar. There were no sounds in the cold night except for the snow crunching under my boots. I could see through the dense trees and brush a single light emanating from Mr. Lukaszewski's side window.

By the time I reached the far edge of the trees, my feet were cold, my lips numb, and my courage diminished. What would my parents say when they found out that I was missing? But I wanted for Christmas a castle made of wood for my tin soldiers, so I stepped out beyond the trees, carefully walked across a small, frozen pond, and nearly crawled to the bottom of Mr. Lukaszewski's window.

I breathed the frozen air, smelled the smoke from a distant chimney, placed my two gloved hands on the windowsill, and slowly pulled myself up so that I could look deep within the house of Santa Claus.

There was Mr. Lukaszewski in corduroy pants, a blue shirt, and suspenders. His old face looked like leather and brown chocolate. He was sitting at a small table, slowly sipping soup in neat, rhythmic motions with a wide, silver spoon, and then he lifted his head and looked right at me. I let go of the windowsill, tumbled backward into the snow, stood up, ran down the driveway, jumped over the small, frozen pond, and nearly dove back into the woods.

I lay flat on my stomach as I heard Mr. Lukaszewski's back door slowly open. I saw his round silhouette as he stood in the weak, yellow light from the small house, which oozed out onto the flat snow. He looked to his right and to his left, and then gave a quick glance in my direction as I lowered my head, wanting to disappear into the snow.

When I heard the door shut, I stayed flat on the ground for a few more moments, just to make sure that I was in the clear. When I carefully lifted my head from under my red wool cap, there to my left were three deer, standing still as sticks, and a buck with a full rack of antlers. If I had been patient, perhaps the rest of the deer would have appeared, quite possibly dragging a red sleigh behind them, but I just ran back through the moonlight between the bare trees, up the path, back onto the porch, and inside the warm kitchen.

When I joined the family in the living room, my father asked me where I was, and I just said, "Out back."

The next time I was sent to buy six eggs for my mother, Mr. Lukaszewski took my coins, gave me an extra egg for free, patted me on the head, and smiled. I smiled too and said, "*Dzieki.*"

That Christmas Eve I placed my cheek against the inside wall of my bedroom and felt the heat that penetrated through the plaster from the brick chimney that rose through the center of the house. I pretended that it was the heat of Santa Claus as he struggled down from the roof and into the living room below, and I thought I could just make out a few Polish words and the jingle of bells, and then I slept in the warm, holy night.

DECEMBER 25

I think how unlikely it is that death is a hole in the ground.
—Mary Oliver

I am a grown man. My children are adults. I could retire. My father is ninety-nine years old. My mother is eighty-nine years old. Suddenly I need reading glasses. Last month I drove out to Mountainside Park at midnight to see if I could observe the meteor shower. I couldn't. Too many clouds.

It is especially dark outside this evening. No moon. Overcast again. Everything is closed up downtown: Sally's bookshop; Rob Jones's hardware; Charles's deli; Annie's sweetshop. All closed. Most houses in my neighborhood are dark. Blinds pulled. No front lights.

Half the world is at war. The Halloween pumpkin is already rotten. Thanksgiving is done. It is supposed to snow this evening, the first snow of the season. We are not built for loneliness, and yet we look out our windows with a longing that we cannot define. This is why I want to explain about the elf that is sitting on my desk, to the left of where I am writing at this moment.

Perhaps it is Santa Claus. He has a hat like Santa Claus: red with white trim. This elf is made of cloth (80 percent polyester, 20 percent cotton), rope, corduroy, and buttons. He is wearing a gingham shirt, a green vest, and red pants with patches.

While Christmas shopping in the HomeGoods in town, I found this elf sitting on a glass shelf. I picked up the Christmas doll, tucked it under my arm, and bought it. The woman at the register looked at me as I placed it on the counter. She smiled. I smiled and said, "For my niece. My *little* niece. She's nine years old."

He is sitting here beside me now. His beard is made of curled yarn. He has two dots for eyes, and a small, red dot of wool for a nose. When I saw him in the store, he made me smile. I am smiling still as I look at the little man sitting across my desk, which is covered with unanswered letters and incomplete manuscripts. There he is, *my* Christmas elf. We need reminders of that place beyond loneliness and loss.

When my younger brother was six and I was eight, he was given a plastic key chain. This key chain was in the shape of an owl. It was red and its eyes were cream white. When we discovered that the owl's eyes glowed in the dark, my brother and I ran to a lamp and placed the owl next to the bright bulb to soak up the light. Next we ran into the closet under the front stairs, closed the door, and looked at the illumination. We laughed and laughed in the closet with the glowing owl.

Then my brother had the good idea of placing the owl right *on* the lightbulb. This way, he thought, the owl's eyes would have an extra glow when we ran back into the closet. Instead, the plastic owl quickly melted into a distorted glob. We never ran into the closet again.

A few weeks ago, for the fun of it, I connected to the Internet, called up the eBay auction page, and typed in "owl key chain." Within seconds there appeared that same owl key chain my brother and I had forty-four years ago. I placed the opening bid, five dollars, and I won two days later. The key chain arrived in the mail today. I quickly pulled out the owl from the mailing envelope and placed it next to the lightbulb in my desk lamp. Then I ran into the closet and closed the door, and I laughed and laughed as I saw the owl's eyes glowing in the dark.

In her poem "Heron Rises from the Dark, Summer Pond," poet Mary Oliver wrote: "I think how unlikely it is that death is a hole in the ground."

I wanted that Christmas elf because my children are gone. I tucked that Christmas elf under my arms because I couldn't see the meteor shower through the heavy clouds. I wanted that Santa Claus because my father is ninety-nine and my mother is eighty-nine, and they still live in the same house where I grew up.

I may need glasses, I may be able to retire, but I can't wait to give my brother that glowing owl Christmas morning. I guarantee that he and I will run to that same closet, close the door, and laugh and laugh. Death is, indeed, more than a hole in the ground.

The world spins in ugliness and death, the pumpkins are rotting, but Christmas, the promise of eternity, exists.

Something very holy happened a little over 2,000 years ago in Bethlehem. If we look inside our own hearts we will quickly discover, still, that Christmas child deep within us all. I don't want a tie or a pair of pajamas for Christmas. I want elves, and Santa Claus, and glowing owls to make me laugh the laugh of the boy, the boy who was given a purity of heart.

That purity of heart exists in us all. I can prove it to you. Come run with my brother and me on Christmas morning as we race into the closet. If you laugh a lot, he may just let you hold the glowing owl for a few seconds.

JANUARY 1

Good parents give their children roots and wings. Roots to know where home is, wings to fly away and exercise what's been taught them.

—Jonas Salk

Once I found a pink moth. Perhaps someone will tell me there is no such thing as a pink moth. There may be no such thing as a flying horse or a gold calf, but I say that once I found a pink moth.

The front door of the large three-story house where I grew up was protected on the outside by four panels of windowpanes, nearly like a greenhouse. Before we entered the house, we had to turn into this small enclosure of glass, wipe our feet, turn the doorknob, and step into the front hallway.

I found my pink moth in this enclosure. It was here that birds often took a wrong turn and flapped their wings in a rush of feathers and noise against the glass, trying to break through the invisible barrier. It was here that spider webs collected and that bees buzzed angrily against the glass as they too were caught in the trap.

One morning—perhaps I was eight or ten—I stepped out through the front door. I noticed another moth desperately trying to find its way out of the enclosure. Each time I found a bee, a bird, or a moth trapped in the porch vestibule, I caught it and let it go. But this insect was a color I had never seen before on a moth: pink, completely pink. I caught the moth and held it in my cupped hands.

What does a boy do with a pink moth? I stepped back into the house, found a shoe box, filled it with grass and a soda cap of water, and placed my moth in the box.

It died, of course. Things cannot be held too long. They need to be set free. I threw the shoe box, the soda cap, and the grass into the garbage can, and I buried the moth in the garden. I feel as though I am always being pulled between wanting to hold on to things and wanting to let them go.

I remember the afternoon my daughter Karen learned how to ride her bicycle alone for the first time. We began in the early fall, Karen and I. I took her training wheels off, but she insisted that I grasp the handlebar and the seat and walk her around the court.

"I'll just let go for a second, Karen."

"No!" she insisted.

Perhaps Karen will be a lawyer someday or a singer. Perhaps she will invent something, make a discovery, give birth to her own daughter. I thought about these things as we wiggled and rattled our way around the block. It didn't take her long to understand how to turn the pedals with her feet. As I held on to the bicycle, Karen's head and dark hair were just to the right of my cheek. She always looked down toward the front of the bicycle, calling out suggestions or laughing a bit.

After a few weeks, Karen was comfortable enough with my letting the handlebar go, but I still had to clasp the rear of the seat.

"Don't let go, Daddy."

Halloween. Thanksgiving. The leaves disappeared. We spent less and less time practicing. Wind. Cold. Winter. I hung Karen's bicycle on a nail in the rear of the garage.

Christmas. One of Karen's favorite gifts that year was five pieces of soap in the shape of little shells, which her mother had bought.

New Year's Eve. Snow. High fuel bills. And then a sudden warm spell.

"Roe?" I said as we woke up. "Do you hear that bird? It's a cardinal. It's been singing for the past ten minutes. Listen." Roe listened. I listened. The children were downstairs watching television.

After I showered, dressed, and ate breakfast, I found Karen in the garage trying to unhook her bicycle. In this last week of January, when it is usually too cold for the children to be outside on their bicycles, it was nearly sixty degrees. I walked into the garage and lifted the bicycle off the nail.

"I love my bicycle, Daddy."

She hopped on as I pushed her across the crushed stones of our driveway to the street. I gave her a slight shove. "Let go, Daddy!" And Karen simply wobbled, shook, laughed, and pedaled off, as I stood alone watching her spin those wheels against the blacktop.

Einstein spoke about time, about the speed of light, and about objects moving beside one another. I wanted to run to Karen, hold the seat of her bicycle, hold on to her handlebars, have her dark hair brush against my cheeks. Instead, I kept shouting, "Keep pedaling, Karen! Keep pedaling!" And then I applauded.

There is no use holding on to the pink moth or your daughter. They will do just fine on their own. Just set them free.

Keep pedaling, Karen. Keep pedaling.

JANUARY 3

People living deeply have no fear of death.

—Anaïs Nin

Every day I leave my house at exactly seven o'clock, and every day, at nearly the same spot on the highway, I meet up with a red truck. It is the same red truck, with dirt clinging onto its back bumper and a backhoe permanently attached to the flatbed. Between the backhoe and the cab of the truck is enough room for three coffin liners.

When I began a new job and found myself on this new route, and when I saw the truck for the first time, I did not know what was being shipped. They looked like oversized coffins. Then I learned that these things are called outer burial containers, or vaults, or concrete boxes. These are placed into the grave first, and then the coffin is placed inside this solid, cement box. Most states do not require the use of outer burial containers, but most cemeteries do.

When a coffin disintegrates underground, it causes the earth to collapse around it, causing a depression in the grass. If a grave is dug next to an old coffin that is not kept in a concrete box, the old coffin will crumble and prevent the next coffin from being placed beside the other.

Every day I pass the truck carrying three coffin liners. I never look inside the truck to see the face of the driver. He is a grave digger. Each morning he is on his way to a cemetery. I think of how he uses the claw of the backhoe to open the earth. I think of the giant teeth biting into the ground, pulling away at the grass, stones, and brown dirt. I think of the earth being scooped up into a pile beside the open grave. I do not know how the man lifts the coffin liner from his truck and lowers it into the hole, but when he is done, the grave is ready for the funeral that day, and I am already at work, making calls, signing papers, typing memos.

In our recorded history, there is only one time that the water of Niagara Falls in New York stopped flowing on its own. On March 29, 1848, an ice jam in the feeding river clogged the falls, completely shutting down the water. People who lived nearby were suddenly startled by the silence, which lasted several hours.

I sit at my little desk day after day, and consider the forty hours of the workweek, the number of vacation days, the sound of the clock. I sometimes place a finger on my neck vein so that I can feel the pulse of my heart.

What is time? When I was a child, time for me was divided between the day and the night. When I was in school, the year began in September. Lately I've come to realize that I am not in a collection of days and months. It seems that the entire year is one day. It seems to me that my entire life is a single day.

I often said to my three children that I could never imagine a life without them. I know that my first son was born when I was twenty-six, so for twenty-six years, he was not in my life— and yet there is no time in my life that I can imagine him not sitting next to me, or laughing, or chasing the dog, or asking to go on the carousel just one more time.

Ancient people believed stones and ferns and trees all possessed a soul, that there was something embedded within the shells and birds and even in the distant moon. But it seems to me that we only begin to live, we only begin to mark time, the moment we realize we are no longer alone, when we are no longer in the desert.

We try to stop time, that gushing force of water raging over the cliff and crashing down into a white, swirling mist. We try to stop time in our memories, wanting things to be as they were, wanting to begin all over again to get it right. And yet we are brave. And we color our hair and spread cream onto the wrinkles of our face. And this afternoon, for the first time in eight years, I passed the grave digger coming home, and his truck was empty.

JANUARY 29

It is not so much for its beauty that the forest makes a claim upon men's hearts, as for that subtle something, that quality of air that emanates from old trees, that so wonderfully changes and renews a weary spirit.

—Robert Louis Stevenson

In this house, I am surrounded by oak trees, some so large that I cannot reach around their trunks and touch my fingers on the other side. In the summer, if you flew over my neighborhood in an airplane, you would only see a rich canopy of leaves, and nothing more. The "tree umbrellas" above my head give me, yes, a sense of protection, but also, depending on my mood, a feeling of confinement.

Perhaps our perceptions of the changing world depend upon our own inner sense of where we are at the moment. When we are sad, we regret the hanging grapevines or the screech of the cicadas. When we are content, we admire the wheat field or the rise of a distant mountain.

My nephew stands in our backyard, and as he looks up to the tall oak trees, he says, "It's like being in a cathedral."

When I was a boy, and my sisters and brother and I were playing the piano, or working out deals in a game of Monopoly, or building space cars with an Erector Set, there came to me sometimes a distant feeling, a longing for solitude, a sadness perhaps. I felt the urge to be alone, outside, beyond the shadow of the house—somewhere inside the woods, tracking rabbits or searching for bird nests.

I remember quitting the Monopoly game, turning in my pink and white money, slipping on my sneakers, and walking toward the back door, through the kitchen, which had a real tin ceiling. My mother was making pea soup. My grandmother and grandfather were sitting at the kitchen table reading the newspaper, sipping their coffee. The white clock on the yellow wall groaned through its little gears, and I said, "Come on, Moses."

Moses was my black cat: long, clever, at ease with the boy calling its name. Moses came into our house because children down the street saved it from drowning. "Would you like a kitten?" they asked, as I bought lemonade from their lemonade stand. "The grocery man was going to drown it." So I brought it home to our cat, which was nursing her own four kittens. "We'll name him Moses," my mother suggested. "Saved from drowning," and the stray kitten quickly began sucking in the life-saving milk of the mother cat.

Now I opened the back door and let Moses out first, and then hurried along the back porch, jumped over the four wooden stairs, and ran into the woods with my black cat, which looked like a steady streak of ink rushing alongside me.

Whenever I entered the woods with my cat, I knew that I would find something wonderful: mushrooms, jack-in-the-pulpits, a woodcock perhaps, deer tracks, a quartz pebble. Sometimes I sat on a rock in the middle of the woods and just listened to the woodpecker jabbing-jabbing into the side of a tree, hunting for ants and grubs, or I'd wait for the Canadian geese to honk on cue as they flew invisibly over the thick shawl of trees.

Once I found a round turtle about the size of a dinner plate. It was on its back, grasping the air with its claws, trying to flip itself over. I stood over the turtle and watched. Moses stepped forward, reached out with one paw, and made a quick jab at the turtle's belly. The turtle pulled in its legs and head. I reached down like a giant, picked up the turtle, and placed it on its belly, then I walked a number of yards to my rock, sat, and waited. Moses joined me, sat at my feet, and began licking his fur and paws.

After a few moments, I saw turtle legs sprout out from under the stable shell. The next minute a turtle head extended from the front of the shell, and then a tail from the back. Moses looked up without any interest. Slowly the turtle began walking in the direction of the swamp, on its way to the water where the geese swam, and where the night frogs sang under the August moon.

Moses and I walked home.

Last night I decided to drive to the supermarket because I wanted to have a roll of film developed. I said to Roe, "I will be back in a half hour." I almost called out, "Come on, Moses."

To reach the store, I had to drive past the airport, a small place for private planes. What I like about the airport is that it is one of the few places in town where there is a horizon. There are no trees to obscure the view.

It was dusk. The red sun spilled her last bit of paint against the western sky. I stopped the car and watched the clouds turn from white, to red, to bronze, and slowly to black as the sun closed in upon itself and disappeared. I felt like pulling in my head and arms, and rolling into the mud on my back, and disappearing into my own shell.

When I drove home, Roe asked me if everything was all right. I said, "Yes, but I could use a back rub."

We went to bed, my wife and I. As I lay on my stomach and her warm hands slid against my tired back, I could see, through the dark, the silhouette of the oak trees; and as Roe whispered, "Just relax, Chris," I closed my eyes, and I felt, again, just fine.

FEBRUARY 14

For this was sent on Seynt Valentyne's day
Whan every foul cometh ther to choose his mate.

—Chaucer

Six hundred years ago in France and England, it was assumed that birds began to mate during the second half of the second month: February 14. It made sense. Spring was not too far off in the distance, and it seemed as if there were more song birds in the woods and fields.

And so began the early and persistent ritual of selecting a sweetheart on Valentine's Day and offering her a token of affection: a kiss, a card, a box of chocolate.

Thirty-five years ago I was a first-year high school English teacher. I taught *Romeo and Juliet* and stories by Truman Capote and O. Henry. My students read *The Catcher in the Rye*, *The Great Gatsby*. The high school play that year was *The Music Man*. Jeanne De Block, the banker's daughter and one of my students, was the star, playing the leading role of Marian Paroo, the librarian.

Jeanne to this day still represents for me all that is good about teenagers: smart, confident, funny. That she also possessed physical beauty and a mature dignity added to her popularity and, over time, created for all who knew her an iconic memory of what we all hope for in our struggles to be loved and to love.

In the fall of 1975, as I stood before my class, I ran down the attendance list:

"Doug?" "Present," Doug called out.

"Wendy?" Wendy waved her hand and smiled.

"Amy?" "Here, Mr. de Vinck."

"Jeanne?" I called, not looking up from my roster. Silence. "Jeanne?" I repeated as I looked up. Jeanne's desk was empty. I marked her absent, finished taking attendance, and began the day's lesson.

By third period, we had heard that Jeanne was in a car accident on the way to school.

By the end of the day, we had heard that Jeanne died.

There was an intersection not far from the high school. A blinking light controlled the traffic. The morning was heavy with fog. As Jeanne properly and cautiously drove through the intersection, another car appeared at her left side and smashed into her, and she died.

Do you remember the film *Witness*, where the people in an Amish village were summoned by a bell because one of their own was in trouble? The men in the fields quickly stopped their work and rushed to the house. People ran down the roads to the sound of the bell. It was like that in the small northern New Jersey village when Jeanne died. Her parents didn't want a wake. They wanted people to come to their home and share in their grief. I will always remember seeing so many people walking up the driveway, up to the house. I will never forget stepping into Jeanne's house and seeing her high school graduation portrait sitting on the piano.

I met my wife on that day, in that house of sorrow, during the mourning for Jeanne De Block, Lady Librarian, the banker's daughter.

I was sitting at the kitchen table, consoling some of the high school students, when Jeanne's sister Linda entered the house with her college roommate, Rosemary—Roe: my future wife, the mother of our three children, the woman who has folded my underwear for thirty-three years, walked with me along the Roman roads in Belgium, swam with me in a beaver pond in Canada.

Our first son, David, was supposed to be born on Valentine's Day. He came two days earlier, on Lincoln's birthday. Today David is a doctor at Columbia University Medical Center in New York City. Our second son, Michael, was born on Jeanne's birthday, March 31. Today he is an EMT and is nearly a paramedic. He wants to be a fireman, perhaps a nurse. And Karen, our daughter—she was just married in September and moved to Portland, Oregon, with her husband Julien. They are in love, on their way, celebrating life and goodness.

The writer Bernard Malamud wrote, "Life is a tragedy full of joy." Roe and I are still friends with her college roommate and with Jeanne's good parents. They know so well that, from their deep sorrow, something wonderful happened: a great love story between Roe and me, the birth of three good people, the continuation of joy born from tragedy.

St. Valentine's Day is a day to celebrate the joys of those we love. Birds select their mates in the early spring; we select our mates in the miracle of circumstances.

Thank you, Jeanne, for my wife and for our three children. Happy Valentine's Day.

FEBRUARY 27

I feel the greatest gift we can give to anybody
is the gift of our honest self.

—Fred Rogers

In 1983, I was working on the pilot for a children's television program that was to include puppets and reading. During the course of my research, I was introduced to Mr. Fred Rogers, creator of *Mister Rogers' Neighborhood.* In the HBO studios in Manhattan, I was brought to what is called the "greenroom," and when the door closed behind me, I was in the room alone with Mister Rogers.

"Hello. I'm Fred Rogers." The tall, thin man wearing a bow tie, blue jacket, glasses, and a smile quickly stood up from a gray, folding chair and extended his hand.

"I'm Chris de Vinck. Hello."

We shook hands and then spoke, for perhaps two minutes, about children's television and my project, but for the rest of the hour, we spoke about our wives, our children; we both opened our wallets and shared pictures of our families. Fred asked me about my writing. I asked him about his music. We laughed a great deal, especially when the producer of the talk show that Fred was to appear in banged loudly on the door and reprimanded me for taking so long with Mister Rogers. After all, the company was being charged by the hour, at exorbitant rates, for the rent of the studio. Fred looked at me in a impish way and whispered, "Oh my. I think we are in trouble."

Two weeks later, when the children were in bed, Roe was in the living room reading, and I was in my small room writing, the phone rang. Roe called from the couch: "Chris. Phone. It's someone called Mr. Rogers."

"Hello, Chris?"

And so began an eighteen-year friendship. Fred invited me to Pittsburgh to be on his television program with him, along with the writer May Sarton. At his home, he and his wife Joanne shared their food, shared the story about how they met at college, and spoke about their mutual love of music.

Fred and I swam in the Atlantic Ocean together, just beyond his small Nantucket summer home, which he called the Crooked House. We sat together at the foot of a large dune, at the very tip of the island, and Fred said, "Right here, Chris, is where my father and I sat so often and spoke about our lives. Right here he told me, often, how much he loved and admired me."

I remember sitting on the deck with Fred at the Crooked House as he was working on a TV script and I was working on my next essay when a large seagull flew down and landed on a post just to my left.

"Hello," said the seagull in a very familiar Fred Rogers' puppet voice.

"Hello," I said.

"Whatcha doin'?" asked the sarcastic bird.

"Working on an essay for *The Wall Street Journal*."

"That doesn't look like work," said the seagull.

"Of course, it's work. Look at that guy sitting over there. What do you think he's doing?"

"You mean that very handsome man laboring over his television program?" the seagull chuckled. Then, in a sudden eruption of feathers, the bird soared above me and flew away. I turned, and there was Fred with a big, seagull smile.

I asked Fred, just then, "How come we became friends?"

"Chris, when I first met you in the studio in New York those many years ago, you didn't want anything from me. You didn't want me to endorse anything. You didn't want my autograph. You weren't impressed that I was Mister Rogers. You seemed to like me for me, Fred, just me."

We attended lectures together at Lincoln Center. We laughed in a taxi when Fred said, "Doesn't God have a sense of humor? As you know, Chris, I am a very private person, and God placed me in a profession that BROADCASTS!" Fred enunciated the word *broadcasts* so loudly in the cab that the driver turned around in puzzlement, and then Fred, the driver, and I laughed and laughed.

I introduced Fred to the writer Henri Nouwen, and Fred and I spent a wonderful four days in Toronto listening to Henri preach to the disabled people at the famous L'Arche community. One night, as Fred and I were walking to the chapel for evening prayers, we spoke about friendship. "The greatest gift someone can give the other person," Fred said, "is his complete honest self."

Fred and I shared, for eighteen years, the honesty of each other, our triumphs and sorrows. Fred asked me to make suggestions on a speech he was preparing for a college in Massachusetts. I asked him to edit a small Christmas novel I wrote. He wept on the phone at the death of his friends. I asked him to pray for my daughter when she was sent to Sloan-Kettering Cancer Hospital.

I believe Fred Rogers was a prophet, a man in possession of profound moral insight and extraordinary gifts of expression.

Once a woman wrote to Fred, saying that she was going through a very difficult time. She was convinced that if she could wear one of his famous sweaters for a while that her sorrows would disappear. A number of Fred's friends tried to discourage him about following up on such a request, but he insisted—"Of course, we'll send her the sweater"—and into the mail the sweater went, with the conviction of his colleagues that the sweater, one among the few that Fred's mother had knitted, was gone forever. However, a year later, the sweater was returned with a note of deep gratitude from the woman. She was better.

Fred personally answered all his letters, extended himself to those in need. He said to the children in his television ministry, "You are special. I like you just the way you are."

Fred was an extraordinary, well-read man: devouring the work of Henri Nouwen, Kathleen Norris, Anne Lamott, the Dalai Lama, Teilhard de Chardin, Rilke, Thomas Merton, and C. S. Lewis—cherishing Antoine de Saint-Exupéry's *The Little Prince.*

We e-mailed each other twice, sometimes three times a day. He liked it that I discovered his name was hidden in the word FRiEnD, and he often signed off on the computer in that manner. He would write that he took a walk in the park near his home and enjoyed the moon. He would tell me about a new book he discovered, or about his grandson coming over for pizza Friday night.

In 1988, Fred invited me to St. James Cathedral in Brooklyn, New York, to be in attendance when he was given the Compostela Award, which celebrated the works of good, holy people who make a difference in this sometimes ugly, sad world. After the award ceremony, Fred and I went to a restaurant for dinner where he said, simply, "Thank you for being my friend. It is hard, Chris, for a public person to have true, close friendships. Thank you for your trust and for your love and for your friendship."

On February 27, 2003, Fred Rogers died of stomach cancer. Twenty-seven days earlier I had received my last e-mail from the man I nearly called father:

> *Bless your heart. I miss you too. I'm really tired, but I must do what I'm required to do (meds around the clock etc.). Someday I hope to be able to tell those who have "sustained" me in such extraordinary ways what their help has meant during the walk (stumble) through this dark valley. Thank you AGAIN AND AGAIN for all your prayers. That's the kind of sustenance I'm needing every*

*minute of every day and night. Love to you and Roe and
the children, as always…and thank you again and again
and again and again…*

your FRiEnD

Thirty-four days after he died, his lawyer sent me a pack-age that contained a note with one sentence: "Fred had a top drawer that had the enclosed marked especially for you. You were truly special to Fred." Inside the package was the large, heavy Compostela Award medallion that Fred had received fif-teen years earlier in celebration of his goodness.

Fred wrote once, "As human beings, our job in life is to help people realize how rare and valuable each one of us really is, that each of us has something that no one else has, or ever will have, something inside that is unique to all time. It's our job to encourage each other to discover that uniqueness and to provide ways of developing its expression."

Celebrate the memory of a man who was rare and valuable, a man who celebrated the essential goodness and purity of heart within each of us, a man who truly believed in a neighborhood filled with people who loved one another.

FEBRUARY 28

Who finds a faithful friend, finds a treasure.

—Jewish saying

There is an old British superstition that if the first thing you say on the first day of the month is "Rabbit! Rabbit!" you will be granted good luck for the next thirty days. If you forget to say the magical word, and you still wish to retain the promise of good fortune, you can repeat the word backward, "Tibbar! Tibbar!" and still keep yourself in the loop of luck.

One evening I was feeling rather low about my publishing career. My agent hadn't been able to sell a recent title, my essays were not being picked up by the newspapers, and, the week before, I had received a letter from one of my publishers stating that another of my books was being declared out of print, which is like sending a racehorse to the glue factory.

I dragged myself around a bit and avoided the word processor, but didn't want to burden Roe with another of my writer's whine about being ignored, underappreciated, and, well, a failure.

"Call Fred," she suggested. She knew the solace a friend can offer. So I called Fred.

"Hello Fred?"

"Hello, my dear. I was just thinking of you."

"I'm a bit discouraged."

"Well, I'm glad you called."

"I thought I'd be a great writer someday."

Fred said in his famous, reassuring voice, "Do you remember what the Little Prince said in Antoine de Saint-Exupéry's little book? 'It is only with one's heart that one can see clearly. What is essential is invisible to the eye.'"

"It seems that my work is invisible to everyone's eyes."

Fred spoke about reaping what we sow. He reminded me that if we work at what we truly love, the work will find its way. When he heard that I was being stubbornly adolescent and not really paying attention to what he was saying, he suggested a different approach.

"Let's play a game." And so Fred introduced me to the rabbit. "You know, Chris, between friends, the one who says, 'Rabbit! Rabbit!' first at the beginning of the month wins good fortune for that entire month. The friend who forgets has to, in surrender, repeat the word backward: 'Tibbar! Tibbar!'"

I liked games. I liked that my sixty-five-year-old friend liked games. We spoke about luck; I shared with him how difficult it had been for Madeleine L'Engle to find a publisher for her famous book *A Wrinkle in Time*. "It was rejected by twenty-six publishers before editors at Farrar, Straus & Giroux read it, loved it, and published it."

"Oh, Chris, it is not luck. Yo-Yo Ma did not become a great musician by luck."

In May 2002, Fred asked me if I would proofread a speech that he was preparing for the Dartmouth graduation. I read aloud Fred's speech over the phone as he followed along. We both had the text in our hands. As I read, I made suggestions and spoke about the use of single words and the delight of his ideas and wisdom. And then I read this: "What is essential about you? And who are those who have helped you become the person that you are? Anyone who has ever graduated from a college, anyone who has ever been able to sustain a good work, has had at least one person and often many who have believed in him or her. We just don't get to be competent human beings without a lot of different investments from others."

I paused for a moment, and then Fred said, "You know, Chris, you have been one of those people in my life."

Each first day of the month, Fred called, and each time he beat me at the game: "Rabbit! Rabbit!" I *never* remembered, and so each time I said, in humble surrender, "Tibbar! Tibbar!"

For me, Fred Rogers was, in many ways, like Harvey, the six-foot invisible rabbit in Jimmy Stewart's famous film.

As the character Elwood P. Dowd in the movie, Stewart says:

"Harvey and I sit in the bars. Have a drink or two. Play the jukebox. And soon the faces of all the other people,

they turn toward mine and they smile. And they're saying, 'We don't know your name, mister, but you're a
very nice fella.' Harvey and I warm ourselves in all
these golden moments. We've entered as strangers.
Soon we have friends. They come over and they sit
with us. They drink with us. They talk to us. They tell
about the big terrible things they've done. And the big
wonderful things they'll do. Their hopes, their regrets,
their loves, their hates. All very large, because nobody
ever brings anything small into a bar."

Fred Rogers was a nice fella. Everyone who met Fred wanted
to tell him about their hopes, regrets, loves, and hates. Fred had
the extraordinary capacity to see the good in everyone he met.

We all need someone to believe in us.

"Keep writing, Chris, from the heart," Fred said often.
"Focus on the invisible."

Fred Rogers died, and now he is my personal Harvey, my
invisible cheerleader, whispering every first day of the month,
"Rabbit! Rabbit!"

MARCH 1

852 million people across the world are hungry.
   —Food and Agriculture Organization of the United Nations

I do not know if we are being watched, or if we are the ones
gawking at life like naive spectators.

Roe and I decided to set up a bird feeder. We bought seeds

and suet bars, and I bought what looked like a small Victorian house that was capable of holding a pound of birdseed at one time. A slot at the base of the house allowed the seeds to filter out as the birds sat on a perch.

Wrens, starlings, cardinals, blue jays, turtledoves, chickadees, red-headed woodpeckers—all of National Geographic—quickly discovered our bird feeder. An added bonus was the arrival of the rabbits and chipmunks that ate the seeds on the ground that fell from the little house, which was hooked onto a black pole. The squirrels were there too, as always, frustrated that we had bought the cylindrical baffle that prevented them from climbing up the pole to the waiting warehouse of seeds.

Yesterday, I noticed that the bird feeder was once again nearly empty. The birds and company were feasting on the last bits of food, so I walked to the closet, opened the door, leaned over, and dragged out the tin canister. As I opened the back door, everything disappeared. The birds flew off in one, quick rush of activity. The chipmunk zigzagged and evaporated into the pachysandra. By the time I reached the empty bird feeder, I was alone, or so I thought.

While pouring the birdseed into the open slot at the top of the little house, I had a sudden realization: I was being watched. The rhododendron branches moved slightly. There was a little rustling sound in the pachysandra. After I hooked the bird feeder back onto the black pole, I walked into the house and stood at the kitchen window, waiting to see how long it took for the birds, rabbits, chipmunks, and squirrels to return. Seconds.

"He's gone," the sparrow must have said with certitude. It seemed as if suddenly every creature knew that the intermission was over, and they could return to the stage.

The woodpecker swooped in, hooked its claws onto the grating that held the suet bar, and began hammering away. A blue jay bullied its way to the perch, rocked its beak back and forth through the seeds, and selected just a sunflower. The seeds that rained to the ground bounced off the head of the chipmunk. The brown rabbit ran out from under the deck, found a spot where the seeds were plentiful, and began chewing and twitching.

They were watching me at the window.

"Will he add more seed? When will he leave?"

This is how a conductor might feel, or a boxer, senator, or movie star. Well, I suddenly felt powerful. I picked up my can of seeds, and I walked out onto the deck again. All the animals quickly scattered back into their hiding places. I walked back into the house and watched. A turtledove fluttered down, nearly bounced to the ground, and quickly began to peck at the seeds. Within seconds, everything once again returned: rabbit, birds, chipmunks. I stepped back onto the deck. They all disappeared. I stood there, trying to see into the dark bushes, trying to find a bird sitting in the oak tree.

I walked back and forth into the house and out onto the deck at least fifteen times, and each time, the birds and squirrels and friends ran off, watched me from their hideouts, then returned once I was safely inside the house.

One last time I stepped out onto the deck with my canister of seeds. I flipped off the lid, dug my two hands deep inside the tin, scooped out handfuls, and just tossed the seeds up into the air like confetti. Then I picked up the canister and flung much of the seeds to the ground surrounding the bird feeder. I felt like flapping my arms and flying up to the top of the oak tree, zooming around the yard, pecking at the newly thrown seeds, turning my head like the rabbit and wrinkling my nose, scratching the ground. But I was being watched. A man has to act like a man: raking the grass, driving to work, sleeping in his house without a perch. I grabbed the tin canister one more time and dumped the remaining seeds in one, wide sweep across the yard.

As I stood inside the house and watched through the

kitchen window, nothing happened for the longest time. The wren probably thought, "That was peculiar. No way for a man to act." The blue jay might have considered the seeds were tainted somehow. "Why would a man fling all that good seed around the yard in such a flourish?"

Fifteen minutes later, a single starling appeared on the grass and began eating the scattered seeds. Within twenty minutes the yard was filled with twenty or thirty birds, a rabbit, four chipmunks, eight squirrels. They found seeds, seeds, and more seeds.

According to the Food and Agriculture Organization of the United Nations, 852 million people across the world are hungry. And according to the Development Program of the United Nations, 1.2 billion people currently live below the international poverty line, earning less than a dollar per day.

I do not know what I am doing as a man. Water gushes out of eight different spigots in my house at a simple twist of the wrist. My refrigerator is filled with healthy grapes, oranges, frozen shrimp, milk, eggs, butter. The cupboards and drawers are stuffed with pasta, bread, sauce, tuna, soup.

Poor nutrition and calorie deficiencies cause nearly one in three people to die prematurely or to have disabilities, according to the World Health Organization.

On the grocery list attached to the humming refrigerator, I wrote "birdseed," and walked away.

Why is it that at *my* house the milk is fresh and the birds are fat?

MARCH 6

World is suddener than we fancy it.

—Louis MacNeice

"Hickory, dickory, dock. The mouse ran up the clock. The clock struck one; the mouse did run. Hickory, dickory, dock."

Slow is the time when we are bored. Slow is the time when we are ill. Fast is the time when we are on vacation. Fast is the time when we are young. "How is it," my neighbor said to me this morning, "that the days are slow, but the years are fast?"

We divide our lives up into bits of time. When we take notice, there is a value in time: last seconds with a departing friend; moments pushing a three-year-old daughter on the swing at the park; savored hours reading the novel *The Great Gatsby*, or the poetry of Louis MacNeice.

When we do not give time reverence and instead squander the days to routine and ingratitude, we do not invest in our capacity to remember. My sister often said, when she was planning a picnic or a hike with her children, that she was creating memories.

One Saturday my son David and his wife Oana were driving on the northbound section of the New Jersey Turnpike on their way to Oana's house for an afternoon visit.

The phone rang.

"Dad?"

"Hi, David."

"We're okay."

"David?"

"We're okay. We were in an accident."

"Is Oana okay? Are you hurt?"

"We're fine. We were driving in the left lane when a car, without any warning, jerked from the center lane into us. We tried to veer to the left, but our car caught the rumble strip and we began to spin."

"David. Where are you?"

"We're here at Exit 8 with the state police. We're okay. When our car started spinning, another car hit us from behind, and *it* began to spin. Our car turned on the highway in a complete circle, and somehow we landed in the right shoulder facing the right direction. The other car spun halfway around and also landed in the right shoulder, but facing the wrong direction. Our two cars were nose to nose. No one was hurt. Our car is completely smashed along the passenger side. I have a scratch on one of my knuckles."

"I'm coming."

"No. It's okay. Oana's mother is already on her way, and we will stay the night. Dad, we were just driving on the highway, and thirty seconds later we are on the shoulder. People stopped. The tires. The metal buckling. The police. All at once."

How do we reconcile the swing of chance with our naive certitude? How do we submit ourselves to events that we cannot control? What if my children's car had flipped over? What if they had hit a tree? David and Oana are both in their fourth year of medical school. How many lives would they have not saved?

Two days later, a sudden news flash was sent through radios and televisions up and down the East Coast. Two tractor trailers collided on the Connecticut Turnpike, and, squeezed between them in this horrific accident, was a car. It was pulverized, almost beyond recognition. The driver was killed instantly.

Fate, time, occasion, chance—these are all subject to the shroud or to the mythic dance around the hot fire of joy. Time is, perhaps, just a line from beginning to end, or a river spilling into the ocean of a future we can hope exists.

Louis MacNeice, in his little poem "Snow," wrote, "World is suddener than we fancy it."

The world newly unfolds with each coming second. Indeed, "to everything there is a season, and a time to every purpose under heaven." One second we are driving on the highway, the next we are disintegrated, or have scratched knuckles.

Do we balance ourselves on the thin line of our existence until we fall, fall, fall, or do we ride the rapids of our lives down to a waiting, open sea?

I feel great joy and hidden guilt that my children exclusively were spared this weekend.

Hickory, dickory, dock.

MARCH 12

Man has survived through tenderness.

—Loren Eiseley

My older brother Oliver died thirty-one years ago today: March 12, 1980. He was a horrible brother. We never did anything together. He never played catch with me. He never advised me about girls. He never slept with me in the tree fort in the woods. He never swapped baseball cards with me or taught me how to fish.

My brother did provide me with some entertaining moments. Because he was blind, I spent many days when I was a boy pretending that I was blind. I'd close my eyes to see how far I could get through the house without knocking anything down. I knew, by heart, where all the doors and chairs were located.

Sometimes Oliver was my Zen guru. He was so quiet. Oliver had no intellect. He'd just lie in his bed like a giant doll. In high school, I'd sit by his side and complain about my poor grades in algebra, or discuss aloud that I liked this girl Linda, but she ignored me, and if I only had a Plymouth Roadrunner she'd pay more attention to me. Oliver would offer no advice in his silence, so it was in that silence where I had to discover my own answers to my woes. Algebra wasn't really important, and Jenny, the new girl, didn't care that I drove her to the high school basketball game in my father's Ford station wagon.

Oliver was for the most part pretty useless. It was my job to feed him dinner: pureed fruit, soup, Beech-Nut baby food in a jar. He couldn't chew. He couldn't hold a fork or spoon in his hand, so I had to scoop up his dinner from the bowl with a spoon and touch it to the tip of Oliver's lips. He'd open his mouth. I'd place the spoon and food into his mouth, and he'd close and swallow. I never split a hero sandwich with my brother. Boys like to do that.

I couldn't even share a drink with Oliver. He couldn't hold a glass either. At dinner I had to lift up his head from the pillow with my left hand and place the rim of the glass at his lips with my right hand, and Oliver drank his milk or water or juice. I never heard him burp. Brothers like to hear each other burp.

When my mother and father and sister and I gave Oliver a bath, you'd think he'd splash his arms up and down for fun in the water. Instead we just slid him into the tub and he'd lie there like large, wet pillow.

Oliver was born with severe brain damage, a puzzlement that the doctors never figured out, but it was clear that Oliver did not have the ability to learn, talk, think, communicate—or dress up like Frankenstein's monster for trick-or-treating, or go sleigh riding with me, or light firecrackers back in the woods without our mother knowing about it. We couldn't be best friends. We couldn't do anything together.

What good was he?

Oliver lived for thirty-two years.

For thirty-two years, I watched how gentle my father was when he shaved Oliver's stubbled face. For thirty-two years, I listened to my mother say to Oliver how much she loved him.

A boy mimics his father and listens to his mother. The great Russian novelist Fyodor Dostoevsky wrote in *The Brothers Karamazov*: "What is hell? I maintain that it is the suffering of being unable to love."

My father taught me how to love Oliver in the way he slowly pulled the sharp razor against Oliver's tender skin. Every morning, for thirty-two years, my mother slowly lifted the white shade of the window that was above Oliver's bed in a manner that was nearly religious, letting in the day's light to spill over my brother's crooked body.

In the evening of the day that Oliver died of pneumonia in my mother's arms, I was in my own home holding my four-week-old son. I was sitting on the couch. The baby was on my lap, kicking his legs, wiggling his arms, looking with great intensity into my own eyes, and I just cried. I pressed my face into the small boy's body and I cried and I cried, and I promised the boy that I would love him for the rest of my life.

The only thing Oliver could do was laugh. You would be walking past his room in the middle of the night, and you'd hear this husky laughter. Perhaps laughter is God's way of reminding us that everything is okay.

The humorist Garrison Keillor wrote, "The highlight of my childhood was making my brother laugh so hard that food came out his nose."

I would have liked to have been able to play that joke on my brother, but in the end, one of the highlights of my own childhood was hearing my brother laugh, and then I'd laugh too.

We did do *that* well together.

Spring

The sun was warm but the wind was chill.
You know how it is with an April day.

—Robert Frost

APRIL 1

Baseball was, is, and always will be to me the best game in the world.

—Babe Ruth

I touched Babe Ruth's baseball bat, one of the bats he used in the 1927 season when he permanently established himself as a home-run hitter with sixty home runs in a single year.

The bat is on display at the Yogi Berra Museum in Montclair, New Jersey. I was tempted to buy a baseball signed by the most famous Yankee catcher, but a friend said, "Don't buy the ball. Just stick around, and Yogi will gladly sign a ball for you for nothing."

Babe Ruth's bat sits in a plastic, rectangular box in the room to the left of the museum. As I entered the room, I glanced at a sign near the box, skimmed it, and jumped to the wrong conclusion. I thought it read: "**PLEASE DO NOT TOUCH BABE RUTH'S BAT**." I quickly said to myself, "Once again, another negative warning." But then I smiled when I realized that I had read the sign incorrectly. It actually read: "**PLEASE DO TOUCH BABE RUTH'S BAT**." And then I noticed a neatly cut hole in the side of the plastic box, which allowed anyone to stroke the handle portion of the bat that once belonged to the most famous baseball player in the world.

I reached in with my left hand and curled my fingers around the base of the bat and thought, "Babe Ruth's hands touched this exact wood, on this exact place as he clobbered his way to fame."

When I was a schoolboy, I would have loved to have run onto the ball field and called out to anyone who would listen, "I touched Babe Ruth's bat!" For a moment I would have been a hero. Some of the guys would accuse me of lying, while others would have wanted to shake my hand. But then someone would yell there wasn't much daylight left, and Brian would take the mound, Doug would set out for shortstop, Len would slip on his father's catcher's mitt, and I would be sent far out to my usual spot, right field, and be ignored for the rest of the game.

Some people do not understand the joy of brushing up again greatness. I bought a copy of my most favorite book, *To Kill a Mockingbird*, which is signed by the author, Harper Lee. I have framed here on my wall a signature of my favorite poet, William Carlos Williams. I like running my fingers on the surface of the signatures and thinking, "Harper Lee devoted six seconds of her life signing this very book," or "William Carlos Williams, one of the greatest American poets, wrote his name on this little piece of paper."

I've been to Robert Frost's grave in Bennington, Vermont, and Walt Whitman's grave in Camden, New Jersey. I visited Mark Twain's house in Hartford, Connecticut, and Pearl Buck's home in Pennsylvania. I loved O. Henry's home in Austin, Texas, and once a year, I walk inside Washington Irving's home in Tarrytown, New York.

I was a shy, unathletic boy. I made it my goal, which I never reached, to climb to the top of every tree in my parent's yard. Some of the maples were four stories high. My greatest triumph was climbing the three-story pine tree and swaying back and forth at the very top, pretending that I could just make out the tip of the Empire State Building. We lived thirty miles from New York City. I could, at least, imagine that I was a hero.

We are drawn to artifacts of greatness. I touched the small sample of moon rock at the Air and Space Museum in Washington,

DC. I loved seeing Dorothy's ruby slippers and Mr. Rogers' sweater in the Smithsonian.

To read a novel by Faulkner makes me feel like Faulkner. To listen to the music of Aaron Copland makes me believe that I, too, can create an *Appalachian Spring* or *Rodeo*.

We are inspired toward faith as we witness the burial of a pope. We are drawn to the election of a new president and are delighted to hear that he likes baseball, just like we do.

Each time I buy a Baby Ruth candy bar, I still anticipate the delicious taste of those nuts, caramel, and chocolate. There is an urban legend that the candy bar was named after the famous ball player. Some historians claim it was named after President Grover Cleveland's daughter, Ruth Cleveland, while others believe it was named after the candy company president's grand-daughter. I still believe that after I eat a Baby Ruth, I can hit a home run, which is what I thought when I was eleven and on my way to the ball field: "If I have a bit of Baby Ruth inside me, maybe, just maybe, I can hit a ball over the pine trees and smash it through a window in the Empire State Building."

Something flutters inside our "inside selves" whenever we see someone famous, or when we hold, for example, a baseball signed by Willie Mays. We feel that perhaps we are a part of it all, in the end.

Walt Whitman believed that the soul was all human beings together forming one soul. It is not Rembrandt admiring Rembrandt, or Charles Dickens reading his books by himself in his library. We feel we are a part of the greatness as we read the novels, see the masterpieces, and listen to the concerts because we *are* a part of the greatness.

I believe a true artist, and a true hero, is someone who opens his arms in a wide embrace, welcoming everyone to come on in and join him. Babe Ruth said, "I won't be happy until we have every boy in America between the ages of six and sixteen wearing a glove and swinging a bat."

APRIL 2

Abbott: *Now, on the St. Louis team, Who's on first,*
What's on second, I Don't Know is on third.
Costello: *That's what I want to find out.*
—Bud Abbott and Lou Costello

Many years ago, on my way to the campus post office on my first day at college, I walked by a little man in a rumpled fedora hat who was sitting alone on a bench. He looked up at me, raised his left hand in a welcoming gesture, and said, "Hello, Yankee boy. A great day for baseball."

Griff was part of the college legend, a man who endured obvious intellectual disabilities and yet who also endeared himself to thousands of students and teachers with his smile and greeting. All he ever said to anyone was, "Hello, Yankee boy," or, "Hello, Yankee girl," and then he'd punctuate his enthusiasm with, "A great day for baseball."

Every day is a great day for baseball, and there is no sport in America that better defines the metaphor for what it is we tend to pursue each day in our sometimes confused and sloppy interpretation of ourselves.

Many years ago, when my son was eight years old, I wanted to spend the day alone with him. I felt that he was being ignored a bit in the family, possibly overwhelmed in school, perhaps annoyed at his older brother's teasing, or his sister's new friends.

I suggested to Michael that we go kite flying at Sandy Hook, the long strip of New Jersey beach that rested under the thick glass eyes of the famous twin lighthouse. "We'll bring the Chinese fish kite." Michael was eager and interested.

We drove down the Garden State Parkway, and quickly found ourselves running onto the beach in a warm, May afternoon. It was the time after the cold winter months and before the summer season. Michael kicked off his sneakers and ran ahead of me while I carried, under my arm, a gigantic, red paper fish.

"Come on, Daddy!" he called out, as he ran into the foam and waves, the last gentle touch of the great Atlantic Ocean unfurling itself at his little feet. I took off my shoes and socks, dropped the kite, and joined my boy.

"The water's freezing," Michael said in cautious delight.

We collected shells and driftwood, found bits of polished sea glass, chased seagulls. Then Michael said, "Let's fly the kite."

As we walked back to the kite and our shoes, he placed his small hand into mine. The wind was strong and steady. We unrolled the fish. I hooked the kite string to its large, open mouth.

"Michael, you take the string. I'll hold the fish by the tail and you start running."

Michael ran and ran as the paper fish quickly filled with air—but no matter how much the wind blew, no matter how fast Michael ran, the stubborn fish would not fly. Only then did I realize that the Chinese fish was not a kite, but a paper windsock, an ornament to be hung on a stick, or down the side of a house for decoration. The fish was never going to fly, and Michael was disappointed.

As I was rolling up the fish, Michael called out from farther up the beach, "Hey! Look what I found." A tennis ball. I looked around where I stood and found a long, smooth stick of driftwood. Michael ran up to me and said, "Dad, see if you can hit."

I could barely hit a baseball, as everyone in my grammar and high school gym classes knew, but did my son also have to know? I swung a few times, lamely hit the tennis ball once, twice, until Michael called out, "My turn."

With each pitch I made, Michael whacked the tennis ball over my head, and then the two of us would race to see who could reach the ball first. A hit at my feet was a single. A hit over my head was a home run. Michael and I played nine innings. We had the beach nearly to ourselves. The waves roared in approval. I kicked the pitcher's mound again and again. Michael took practiced swings with his driftwood bat. He won the Pennant and the World Series.

My son is a graduate of Rutgers University and is now a paramedic. What does a man say to his son as the boy becomes a man? Santiago, the old fisherman in Ernest Hemingway's classic little book, *The Old Man and the Sea*, said to Manolin, his adolescent protégé, "Have faith in the Yankees, my son. Think of the great DiMaggio."

Hemingway admired DiMaggio's gumption to overcome physical injury and roar back to a winning season in 1946. The old man in the novel admired DiMaggio's courage. "I would like to take the great DiMaggio fishing," the old man said. "They say his father was a fisherman. Maybe he was poor as we are and would understand."

DiMaggio understood suffering and endured. Another famous Yankee, Lou Gehrig, stood before thousands and thousands of people in Yankee Stadium on July 4, 1939. Accepting the diagnosis of his fatal disease, he said, "Fans, for the past two weeks you have been reading about a bad break I got. Yet today, I consider myself the luckiest man on the face of the earth."

Baseball is the great American symbol for what it is that we try and do each day: step up to the plate and swing with the hope that we hit a home run over the heads of our fathers. Baseball makes us feel lucky. Have faith in the Yankees, I tell my son. Have faith in yourself.

I think that the giant paper fish is still rolled up in the attic somewhere.

Hey, Yankee boy. Hey, Yankee girl. Today *is* a great day for baseball.

APRIL 3

There are no ordinary moments.

—Dan Millman

The world can be a sudden place. We can work through our daily routines that spill over into weeks and months, and little happens—but then a quick incident adds an exclamation point to the quiet narrative of our lives.

A few days ago, I drove to the library to return a number of CDs: classical music that I admire, especially Bach's *Brandenburg Concertos* and *Orchestral Suites*. As I walked out of the library, I was surprised to see how quickly the skies had darkened, and how powerfully the wind suddenly whirled down into the small valley where I live. By the time I reached my side of town, rain, leaves, and small broken branches were pelting the car's windshield. The temperature dropped twenty degrees. The cold front had arrived.

Just as I stepped into the house, the clouds split open, lightning illuminated the yard, thunder exploded, trees bent back and forth in their wild sway. I looked out the kitchen window, and said to myself how impressed I was that so many twigs and leaves had so quickly covered the back lawn, and then I heard a distinctive crack.

I turned my head slightly to my right and witnessed a gigantic branch crashing down on the garden furniture, smashing the glass table and shredding the green cloth umbrella. The flower boxes were swept upside-down; the lawn chairs were blown to their sides. It was as though a madman had rushed through the backyard with vengeance and a club, destroying everything he could touch in twenty-five seconds.

Of course, the insurance company will not replace the garden furniture because I have a $500 deductible. It always amazes me that we can buy insurance that doesn't insure. But I was reminded by this sudden storm to appreciate the calm and stable days. I spend too much time dreaming about the way things could be rather than celebrating what is. Someone recently suggested that I should learn to desire what I have. I am more and more open to accepting the little surprises in my life rather than hoping for grand luck.

So when someone suggested that I go to the racetrack last Saturday, I thought to myself, I've never seen a horserace. I've never placed a single bet anywhere in my life. I'll make my own adventure and break from the routine of my life on my own terms.

"Sure," I said to my friends. "I'd like to go to the track."

This track is near the New Jersey shore and is one of the oldest and finest horse-racing arenas in the state. I knew nothing about betting. I learned the difference between two dollars to "show" and two dollars to "place." I liked the sound of the horses tromping down on the track during the race. The sky was blue. The flowers were in full bloom hanging from the stadium, decorating the front concourse. I ate a hot dog, placed bets on eight of ten races, and at the end of the day left the stadium in the black with $2.60.

Before the seventh race, I was standing in the crowd, checking the program, smiling at the cigar-chewing, hard-core bettors sharing information. As I tried to lean over and see if I might pick up some useful tips, one of the race horses, right before us on the track, reared upward, kicking its two front legs high above everyone, the way Roy Rogers' horse, Trigger, did on the famous television program. The attendant and the jockey—who was not on the horse at the time—held onto the reins, trying to soothe the animal. The horse stood for a few seconds, then once again reared upward violently and kicked its legs in the air again and again, and then fell over onto its back, then to its side, and began violently kicking its legs again and again and again. Then all was still. The horse was dead.

Within minutes there was a man with a stethoscope. An animal ambulance arrived. Attendants placed a wide, tall, black curtain in front of the dead animal so that we could not see the horse being dragged into the large truck. There was no announcement, except that the horse had been taken off the roster. No mention of the horse's dying. No mention in the newspapers the next day that a race horse had died. Let's keep it a secret. Let's not smudge the reputation of the race track. Everything is pretty. Flowers are in bloom. Bet your heart out. Have a hot dog. Tra-la-la-la-la.

At the circus of our lives, we walk the tightrope. We can balance plates on the tips of long sticks, and dangle in the air with an umbrella in our hands, maintaining our equilibrium against the fall. We can feel confident, but then the line breaks, or the fear sets in, and we tumble down, down, down to the net, if there *is* a net, and regain our composure.

A branch crashing, a horse in its death throes, little hints of a grievous world, victims to natural disasters, and sudden death....We send people into space, ignore the hungry, wage war, pay the bills, eat chocolate doughnuts.

I could be a pirate, or a famous writer, or an ordinary man who bets on horses and cleans up the backyard after a storm. Tra-la-la.

APRIL 4

A thing of beauty is a joy for ever.

—John Keats

Over 40,000 years ago, respected elders crawled deep inside dark caves, in what is today southern France, and drew bison and antelope on the walls using crushed clay and hematite. Today the cave paintings are considered some of the most beautiful images of primitive art we human beings have ever created.

Sei Shōnagon, a servant to the Japanese Empress Sadako 1,000 years ago, wrote a single volume, *The Pillow Book*. It is difficult to classify: some call it a diary, others a collection of snippets and essays. It is a book that reveals the clever, innocent, haughty, humorous, wise thoughts of a woman living ten centuries ago.

Under the heading "Elegant Things," Shōnagon lists "duck eggs, shaved ice mixed with liana syrup and put in a new silver bowl; wisteria blossoms. Plum blossoms covered with snow; a pretty child eating strawberries."

We like to preserve hints of beauty, whether in dark caves or illuminated inside the pages of a book.

For my tenth birthday, my grandfather gave me a Morgan silver dollar. It was the size of my ear, heavy in my hand, and tarnished. My father suggested that I use my mother's silver polish on the coin, so I rummaged around inside the kitchen pantry until I found the squat tin that contained a pink, hard substance; I also found the small polishing rag.

I wrapped my index finger around the rag, dipped it into the tin, and collected a small dollop of the smooth polishing cream. I felt like a treasure hunter as I slowly ground the silver polish in a circular motion onto the surface of the cold coin, and slowly the image of Lady Liberty transformed itself from a gray, dull silhouette to a bright, silver Madonna. The coin was beautiful.

"A thing of beauty is a joy for ever; its loveliness increases, it will never pass into nothingness," the poet John Keats reminded us. Beauty once created is, we believe, forever indelibly stamped on the surfaces that we preserve, including our own faces.

When I was a boy, each morning my ninety-year-old grandmother stood before her mirror like a model from a Vermeer painting. I liked watching her pinch a small puff of cloth between her fingers and lightly pat it in pink face-powder, which she gently applied to her Grand Canyon wrinkles. Then she would smile. It was the smile that I remember and her teasing turn as she quickly tapped my nose with her facial pad, and I moaned in feigned disgust.

Physical beauty is, in the end, ephemeral. Caves and paint wear out; books fade; our faces give way to age and dryness.

Michelangelo's famous paintings on the ceiling of the Sistine Chapel in Rome were covered with candle soot, grease, and dust for five hundred years until 1980, when the Vatican dared to consider cleaning the art and restoring it to its original luster. But the soot and dust continue to rise; the grease continues to seep into the paint and the brush strokes.

The evidence of true beauty is not found in the artifacts we create to express such beauty. Beauty is found in the smile of the creator.

Each spring, Roe and I plant red, pink, purple, and white impatiens in clay pots. Throughout the summer, they thrive under the shadows of the oak trees, adding color and a small splash of beauty to the garden. Just before the first frost, I drag a single pot of impatiens into my room, here where I write. Throughout the winter, the flowers continue to bloom, and the leaves lean toward the window. Each time I walk into this space to write, or when I close the lights for the evening, I look at the flowers and smile, knowing that I was able to preserve, for a small bit of time, a moment's beauty—the same moment my grandmother preserved as she smiled in the mirror. It was the same delight I felt when I polished my silver dollar; the same eagerness Shōnagon must have felt when she held the duck eggs in her unblemished hands; the same magic the shamans must have recognized under the glow of their yellow torches when they drew images of wild beasts running along the walls of eternity.

Beauty, Keats wrote, will keep us "full of sweet dreaming, and health, and quiet breathing," and, in spite of our age, in spite of the recognition of our personal sorrows, "in spite of it all, some shape of beauty moves away the pall from our dark spirits," and we have the glow of the sun, the moon, a tress of hair, simple sleep, daffodils, bison, plum blossoms, all giving us a moment's pause to smile and to acknowledge that, yes, *we* are beautiful.

Won't you come with me today and polish a silver dollar?

APRIL 5

Weeping may endure for a night, but joy cometh in the morning.
—Psalm 30:5

For the last thirty years, I have been writing books, essays, and poetry, and from the very beginning, I was determined to celebrate the combination of joy and sorrow in such a way that is neither sentimental nor harsh.

Too much of what is published today is either corny and predictable, or nasty and crude. For myself, I have found that the richest material for my writing can be discovered in the confidence that we human beings are happiest when we learn how to identify and accept the combination of our joys and sorrows.

In my work, I have been cautious about overtly speaking about goodness. Such candid sharing of something that can so easily be perceived as naive not only diminishes what it is that I want to write, but it also diminishes the reader, because we have been poisoned in our culture to believe that crassness, vulgarity, and harshness are elegant, on the cutting edge of wisdom, and that what is charming, delightful, and possibly even good is sentimental slop.

Attempting to make cultural changes based on ego and false talent often produces ugliness. Attempting to be avantgarde speaking about what is lovely and sweet often produces lollipop logic and frilly nonsense. But art that endures, art that moves a people to broader wisdom, is created in the context of history and blossoms from the innate gift of the artist.

I wrote a small poem this evening, "Choosing Melons at the Market," claiming that the best of our human existence can be discovered in the simple gesture of buying melons and fish in the town square. In this poem I suggest that our world is not made of stone, that hard, gray substance hurled again and again around the burning sun.

I believe the center of our world can be compressed into the beauty of a single rose. We human beings have been given a promise by historians and prophets that the center of our existence is not death or angry articles in the newspaper.

Perhaps you believe that the world is on fire. Yes, we have horrible earthquakes and cyclones. Yes, we have nations starving and suffering the repression of dictators and greedy politicians. So what do we do—just agree that the world is a cesspool? No. I suggest that each day we walk out to the garden or to any place where roots freshen the earth.

The garden is our own lives, where we have been planted by circumstances. In that garden I suggest that we seek a place where we can plant what we are given. We are like roots, filled with potential to grow. We can freshen the earth with our existence. We can take this earth that has been given to us at birth and freshen the soil and create something beautiful.

I do believe that each day we are given a new paradise and a chance to write our story again. I believe that we can bless our innocence, bless those who choose peace, bless the sparrow and the birches, and bless those who suffer.

In the glory of goodness, in the glory of beauty exposed in the market, when the moon illuminates the darkness and does her part, we can promote the promise of goodness. We can promote that beauty is never dead. We can be a people who simply walk to the market and choose melons, who do good work, and who find our way home.

It has been my theory that goodness pursues goodness. Is that a sentimental, corny idea? Will I ever be a Walt Whitman, a man who dramatically changed the way that we look at our American culture?

I just want to be a man who buys fish from the fishmonger, who freshens the earth, and who accepts beauty and sorrow combined. I just want to share the news that paradise is indeed waiting for us each morning.

All I want to do is invite you to read my little poem, and then afterward share with me a slice of sweet melon.

Choosing Melons at the Market

In the glory of goodness, in the glory of beauty,
Among the sound of sorrow, exposed in the market,
So too when you sleep and are not aware,
When the moon illuminates the darkness and does
    her part,
There, in your fingertips, there when lips are held
    together
And breath or silence sustains you in silence
That you may not understand a holy refrain,
There, once and forever, there beyond the sound of water,
Clearly marked as the stars are marked in the shape of
The bear or lute, not hope, not courage, more a solid
    form
Or a gesture as you open the door for the day.

A promise is given, a promise to be discovered in the
    center,
All brought to the rose in recognition, after all. Not death,
Not anger, not fear in a locked room or stories in the
    newspaper
That try each day to define gloom and importance.

Walk out to the garden, or to any place where roots
    freshen the earth,
When sky is defined in light and eagerness for the new
    rotation.
See? The world is not on fire. Blessed are the innocent.
Blessed are those who choose peace. Blessed are the
    sparrows
That are exposed in the birches. Blessed are those
    who suffer.
Blessed are those who stand to defeat and rake the leaves.

Each day is a new paradise, each day a chance to write
the story again.
There is a beginning and there is no end.
Beauty born is not beauty's death. Glory born is glory
at rest
In the silence of the tombs in memoriam.
Glory are the dead. Glory are the people choosing
melons,
Wishing the fishmonger a good day, finding their
way home
After the market. The world is not made of stone.

APRIL 8

I am lonely, lonely.
I was born to be lonely,
I am best so!

—William Carlos Williams

On April 8, 1974, as I was skimming through *The New York Times*,
I read a headline that caught my attention: *The Rewards of Living a
Solitary Life*, by May Sarton. I had no idea who May Sarton was,
but I knew that I was a lonely graduate student at Columbia
University, with thoughts of becoming a Catholic priest or a Peace
Corp volunteer, neither of which, of course, defined my own
inexplicable turmoil.

At twenty-three, I had no way of knowing what Sarton
meant when she wrote in the newspaper that day: "Alone we can

afford to be wholly whatever we are, and to feel whatever we feel absolutely. That is a great luxury."

Luxury? I didn't think that a celibate life or a year living in a foreign country helping people build mud hunts would be a luxury, so I *didn't* take Robert Frost's advice: I chose the road *most* traveled. I took a job right after college, married well, raised three children, worked steadily for thirty-two years as a high school English teacher and school administrator, and all along the way I grappled with the savage crocodile of loneliness that snapped at my feet again and again.

We struggle with two selves: the public self among our wives and husbands, friends and children, and the private self arguing with that contentious being looking back at us in the mirror.

"Why isn't marriage enough?" we ask. "How is it that the love of our children doesn't satisfy?" we think. "I could have been a contender. I could have been somebody," we say, as we imitate Marlon Brandon in his famous role as a failed prizefighter in the fabled film *On the Waterfront*.

Too often when we are tired or discouraged, we fall into loneliness, and then all the demons of failure or lost dreams creep in and attempt to strangle us.

Many years after I found that essay in the newspaper, Fred Rogers and I became close friends, and he introduced me to May Sarton. May, Fred, and I sat together on the famous swing on Mr. Rogers' porch in his make-believe television neighborhood, and ever since that moment, May and I were friends. For ten years we corresponded, shared our published books, and understood the demands of each other's regular life pressing upon our writer's ego.

I visited May a number of times at her home in York, Maine, a house that sat up on a small hill overlooking her famous garden and the Atlantic Ocean.

It was May Sarton who cooked for me my first live lobster. We drank wine together, and as she drove me to a restaurant, she said, "Look, Christopher, all the lilies of the valley. There!" And she pointed to the side of the road. "How I love the lilies of the valley."

I remember May telling me how grateful she was to the poet Archibald MacLeish. "He was very kind to young writers, and I swam with him in his pond at his home in Conway."

May loved her cats, her correspondence, her lovers, her friends, especially Juliett Huxley. She loved Yeats, and she loved me. We sat on her couch many times and read poetry to each other: things she had just written, things I had just written. She wanted to know about my wife and children, and she encouraged me to keep writing, often saying in her letters that she longed for news from me and hoping that I had a little time for myself to write.

May was delighted that my parents were born in Belgium because she too was born in Belgium, and remembered the lush, European clouds against the blue, blue sky. May also loved that my birthday was August 3 because that was that day of her mother's birth.

The wonderful Jewish philosopher Martin Buber wrote, "I do, indeed, close my door at times and surrender myself to a book, but only because I can open the door again and see a human face looking at me." And my favorite poet, William Carlos Williams, wrote in his famous poem "Danse Russe": "I am lonely, lonely. I was born to be lonely, I am best so."

May Sarton—poet, novelist, essayist, feminist—helped me resist the temptation to abandon loneliness. She wrote in the newspaper that day, "Alone one is never lonely: the spirit adventures."

And yes, I agree that a writer's life demands, in part, a monastic environment, but he also needs fresh lobster, the whisper of his lover beside him, the dance, the Belgian clouds, swimming in Conway, lilies of the valley.

We are all contenders, battling the secluded self in the midst of the spirit's adventure.

APRIL 10

We must make the world honest before we can honestly say
to our children that honesty is the best policy.

—George Bernard Shaw

The phone rang. "Dad. I got into a slight car accident. What should I do?" "Are you OK? Are you hurt? Is anyone hurt?"

"No, no. Everything is fine," my son, a student at Rutgers University, said in a calm, reassuring manner. "I was backing out of a parking space and wasn't paying attention. I hit the rear bumper of a car. I cracked it and pushed it in a bit. There was no damage to my car."

"Michael, just call the police on your cell phone. Wait for someone to come. They will take care of it."

Forty-five minutes later, Michael called back. "Dad, the policeman came. He was a nice guy. I showed him the damage to the other car, and as he and I were looking at the cracks and paint, the couple who owned the car walked up to us."

Michael said that he apologized to the couple. "Yeah. It was my fault," he said to them. "I was in a hurry. I just backed up into your car."

Then Michael said to me, with a hint of amazement, "The woman—she looked at the dented bumper, looked at me, then said, 'This car has been such a curse. That bumper was hit a long time ago. You didn't cause the damage.'"

The woman's husband said to my son, "I admire that you waited for us and didn't drive off."

The policeman said to my son, "See what happens when we do the right thing?"

Michael said that everyone shook hands. Everyone was gracious, and honest, and I was amazed.

Reflecting on it in bed that night, I said to Roe, "I am amazed how well that incident went with Michael today. He didn't drive off without telling anyone. The policeman was not rude, arrogant, or condescending. The woman did not try to pin the damage on Michael and his insurance company."

"But, Chris," Roe reminded me, "that is how things should go. Isn't it sad that we are so trained these days to accept that wrong, nasty behaviors are the norm and that goodness is out of the ordinary?"

We've had presidents and vice presidents who have manipulated the truth. The airline industry boldly advertises wonderful, discount fares, only to tack on expensive, extra costs, printed at the bottom of the ad in a despicably tiny font. Talk shows and reality television are replete with people humiliating each other. Evening police shows and news programs openly display murder, rape, gore, and violence simply to win over audiences and charge higher advertising rates. Best-selling fiction lists are dominated by murder plots. Pharmaceutical companies entice doctors to prescribe their products by using slick, young sales reps bringing lunches, smiles, and handshakes to the doctors' offices.

Ice-cream containers are getting smaller and their prices are increasing.

Salesclerks complain more and more about the rudeness of customers.

The American car industry cries because of its self-inflicted wounds, as it sells inferior cars at superior prices.

The tobacco industry continues to trick people here and abroad into buying products that it knows will kill people.

Yes, I have become a cynic, a man who believes that goodness is becoming more and more the exception.

My mother was a teenager during the four years of Nazi occupation of Brussels. When American troops poured into the streets of Brussels at the end of the war, all the church bells in the city rang for the first time in four years. America was the world's hero. Innovation was the bold engine that propelled the United States to the moon.

Our environment was lauded and protected by the government. Dams were built. National parks increased in number. Affordable, well-built homes were constructed. Jobs with secure wages, health benefits, and pensions were plentiful.

The United States is in deep trouble. We are not a nation that is united, as was promised by the last administration. We are not a nation creating goods and services based on the foundation of integrity and value. We are not a nation conducting a meaningful dialogue with the rest of the world.

Goodness is not in fashion these days. Honesty is looked upon as a naive roadblock in the business community. The bottom line in our economic system is not customer satisfaction and product integrity, but profit. We try to make money by creating the most amount of profit with the least amount of investment and material. We ship jobs overseas, and in the neighborhood we create homes built with particle board.

It is a sad thing when a father goes to bed at night pleased that a college student, a policeman, and a young couple didn't argue, cheat, run away, lie, maneuver, posture, gouge, or shoot their way out of a situation.

A father ought to go to sleep each night knowing that his son is living in a country that will not try to take advantage of him each day of his life.

Where is that America?

APRIL 12

We're fools whether we dance or not,
so we might as well dance.

—Japanese proverb

On my way home from work, as I was listening to WQXR, the
New York City classical radio station owned by *The New York
Times*, I heard a piece of music: "The Red Queen's Gavotte." I
thought that I was listening to the orchestra of the gods. The little piece began with an invitation, etched in the air with trumpets and violins, to sway, or to dance, or to pick up an invisible
self and dance along the highway. I was tempted to stop my car,
hold up my hands and stop the traffic, and say, "Listen! Listen to
this music! It is that beautiful." I would have been taken for a
"Mad Hatter" for sure.

There is a thrilling movement throughout the music of
Irving Fine. I did not know this was the composer until his name
was announced at the end of the recording. "'The Red Queen's
Gavotte,'" the commentator stated, "was created by Irving Fine
as incidental music for *Alice in Wonderland*."

The entire rendition suggests a royal delicacy that the
Queen of Hearts did not deserve, but in the music, too, there is
a sense for charm and beauty that compelled Fine to combine
musical instruments to his own sensitivity that, simply, graces
the human heart with a clear sense for significant goodness.

Lewis Carroll's Queen of Hearts was a comical figure,
shouting, "Off with her head! Off with her head!" The silly King
pretended to comply, but then noticed Alice talking.

"Who ARE you talking to?" said the King, going up to Alice, and looking at the Cat's head with great curiosity.

Poor Alice. How do you explain to a king that you are talking to a Cheshire Cat that is sometimes invisible? How could I possibly begin speaking to people in their cars about this little piece of music that I just heard?

"It's a friend of mine—a Cheshire Cat," said Alice: "allow me to introduce it."

"I don't like the look of it at all," said the King: "however, it may kiss my hand if it likes."

"I'd rather not," the Cat remarked.

"Don't be impertinent," said the King, "and don't look at me like that!" He got behind Alice as he spoke.

"A cat may look at a king," said Alice. "I've read that in some book, but I don't remember where."

"Well, it must be removed," said the King very decidedly, and he called the Queen, who was passing at the moment, "My dear! I wish you would have this cat removed!"

The Queen had only one way of settling all difficulties, great or small. "Off with his head!" she said, without even looking round.

"I'll fetch the executioner myself," said the King eagerly, and he hurried off.

I felt compelled to stop my car and sit on the side of the highway and explain to commuters that the Cheshire Cat is always listening to us, and queens are hotheads, and kings do not deserve to have their hands kissed, and there is this piece of music created by Irving Fine that defines a lyrical nature discovered in our invisible selves that is recognized by others when we offer our own Cheshire Cat smile.

I do not know much about Irving Fine. He taught at Harvard and had three daughters, I believe. Leonard Bernstein wrote about him:

> True charm is one of the most difficult things to achieve musically; and Fine has achieved it simply and honestly revealing the man in the music. In [his music] we can behold a personality: tender without being coy, witty without being vulgar, appealing without being banal, and utterly sweet without ever being cloying. Such a man (and such a work) is rare enough to cause rejoicing.

These are the things that I heard in Fine's "The Red Queen's Gavotte." A gavotte is a kissing dance that originated in the sixteenth century. It was a French peasant dance created by the inhabitants of Gap (Gavots) in the Dauphiné province in southern France. You had to skip, then raise your feet like in a little march. The first couple kissed each other, then they had to kiss everyone else in the room.

> *"Off with her head!" the Queen shouted at the top of her voice. Nobody moved.*
> *"Who cares for you?" said Alice, (she had grown to her full size by this time.) "You're nothing but a pack of cards!"*
> *At this the whole pack rose up into the air, and came flying down upon her: she gave a little scream, half of fright and half of anger, and tried to beat them off, and found herself lying on the bank, with her head in the lap of her sister, who was gently brushing away some dead leaves that had fluttered down from the trees upon her face.*

And then Alice woke up from her tremendous dream. We are cuddled to dream and weep and so to dream again as we are lured by saints or white rabbits to hope for a good tomorrow. In the music that we love, we are brought to that place where we kiss and dance and tease the Cheshire Cat.

Let's kick down the stack of cards, stop on the side of the highway, and listen closely to Irving Fine's little Gavotte together—and remind ourselves that we are tender, witty, appealing, and utterly sweet.

APRIL 17

"I find television to be very educating. Every time somebody turns on the set, I go in the other room and read a book."

—Groucho Marx

Often, when I walk through the streets in my small New Jersey village, I ask myself, "Where are all the children?" The yards are empty, and the parks are abandoned. It is as though I were walking through the little town of Hamelin, Germany, in the thirteenth century, and all the children have been lured away to the mountain cave by the famed Pied Piper.

When I was a child, and the wisteria vines curled up the sides of the house like giant ropes, the summers were long, and my sisters and brothers and I were always up for a game of SPUD, or for a race on our bikes, or for a trip to town to buy Ring Dings or Devil Dogs.

Sometimes our neighbors—Johnny, Patty, Marie, Walter, and Paul—joined us in our adventures, and the ten of us built grass huts, searched for goldfish and turtles over by the swamp, stuck lilacs in our hair, and pretended the long rhododendron leaves were dollar bills as we bought "gas" for our bicycles at the gas station, which was more often used as the mailbox.

Often, our times as children were used debating the activities for the day: playing Monopoly, building paths in the woods, climbing the maple tree, and pretending we were on a train speeding to Boston. The apple tree was an elephant with red spangles carrying us to India for the afternoon.

We turned the old chicken coop into a bakery, a bank, a fort, a pirate ship. My brother built a miniature cable car and strung it down a long slope, which allowed us to deliver messages back and forth. We built tree forts, campfires (good for baking potatoes). We cut out "houses" inside the mock orange bushes. We found natural clay in the woods, rolled it into little bowls, which we fired in the campfire, and painted their sides with red, blue, and yellow paint.

In the evening we were told stories about Baba Yaga. We read, rolled marbles back and forth in the upstairs hallway, created a circus in the attic where the cat was trained to follow a string and climb over the pile of Christmas boxes. Or we ran in the dark, catching fireflies, playing hide-and-seek, or laying on our backs, pointing to the stars and creating our own constellations. "Those stars look like my hand," or, "Over there. They remind me of scissors."

According to the National Institute on Media and the Family, children spend more time watching television than any other activity except sleeping.

The American Academy of Pediatrics discovered that in a year, the average child spends 900 hours in school—and also sits nearly 1,023 hours in front of a television, witnesses 200,000 acts of violence by age 18, and sees 40,000 commercials each year.

Researchers at Johns Hopkins University School of Medicine, and experts at the National Institute of Health, conclude that childhood obesity is out of control and is directly linked to the amount of time children spend sitting in the glow of the television.

There are no statistics, no research, that claims the value of television outweighs, on any level, the great harm it does to children's bodies and minds.

Children these days aren't being led astray by the Pied Piper. The famous rat catcher hasn't extracted children from the streets and fields of our country. Television has done that with its own, sad allure.

MAY 5

Everything being a constant carnival, there is no carnival left.
—Victor Hugo

There was a time when a real carnival came to town. There were clowns and cotton candy, snow cones and Ferris wheels, dancing bears, men on stilts, fire-eaters, balloons, bumper cars, corn dogs, jelly, quilts, honey, an auction over at the firehouse, cider, men in jeans and boots strolling down the midway with their wives and girlfriends.

Children held dimes in their hot, little hands, or tossed ping-pong balls into fish bowls. Just as the sun was done for the day, strings of light illuminated the dunking booth. Eerie wails emanated from the haunted house, and there were rumors of fireworks and a raffle for a brand new Chevy.

We worked at our entertainment. Time was, the whole town contributed to the festivity: the high school teachers set up a booth selling candy apples and bookmarks; the mayor promised to donate his pocket watch at the auction; the children over at the Central Baptist Church sang in the gazebo every half hour.

The magic of those days seems dead. Does a boy wake up in the morning anymore hoping to lash his leg to Sandi Kellerman and compete in the three-legged race? Do grandfathers squeeze fifty-dollar bills into the palms of their sons and daughters with the words, "Take the kids to the carnival tonight. I'll pretend I hear them laughing."

America was a fiddle-playing, moon-catching place once, where hayrides were better than a trip on Cleopatra's barge, and custard ice cream was a plump, rich treat at the peak of a crisp wafer cone.

Carnivals these days seem to be nothing but traveling money traps. Trucks pull into church parking lots and set up whirl-a-gig rides that clank and bump. The man at the Ferris wheel, with a rag hanging from his back pocket, doesn't smile. The plastic horses at the carousel don't seem to have the ability to trot, or race, or even just carry the children to the moon and back.

Somehow we've lost the ability to recreate a childlike awe into the way we have fun these days.

When I was a boy, between carnival seasons, my sisters and brothers and I created our own world of gypsy dances and puppet shows. My sister cajoled our tomcat to be a Bengal tiger and chase a string up and down the front porch steps, and then she'd charge us a dollar a show. A dollar was a rhododendron leaf. Five dollars was the leaf of the mock-orange bush. I was the tightrope walker, balancing myself along the branch of the maple tree. Anyone who had a bicycle could join the parade from the mailbox to the garage and back. We wore lilacs in our hair, shared orange Kool-Aid on the back porch, hung balloons, sang cowboy songs, and we all just felt fine at the end of the day.

Why are carnivals so bland these days? Why are the rides so expensive and the ice cream so watery?

I want to buy a barn filled with pink cotton candy for a quarter. I want to be a Cub Scout and call over to my friend Jake and challenge him to a bean-bag toss and race him to a carousel that has real music played by mechanical drums and horns run by steam.

I want to dangle upside-down from a maple tree and charge my sister three rhododendron dollars if I do a flip onto the ground, and I'll treat her to a ride in the wheelbarrow for an extra mock-orange leaf in our carnival yard where the sun stays for a while, and we turn ourselves into clowns and children.

Where are the carnivals?

MAY 10

"What a piece of work is a man! How noble in reason!
How infinite in faculty!…In apprehension how like a god!"

—Hamlet

Yesterday I took a ferry to New York City to have lunch with my editor at the *Wall Street Journal*. Ever since 1984, Barbara has edited every piece I have written for the newspaper. She is smart. She loves her family. She can speak about the central issues of the day as if she were right there in the middle of it all. Barbara defines, with ease and accuracy, positions of substance and even grace on a regular basis.

Barbara wrote movie reviews, play reviews, and edited many of the most respected writers, politicians, CEOs, and entertainers in the last twenty years. Barbara wrote many of her own essays for the Op-Ed page. She is tall. Her hair is long and brown. Her smile is genuine and lovely. New York City.

I drove to Liberty Park, the nationally recognized grounds that claim Ellis Island and the Statue of Liberty, in order to take the ferry into the city. Imagine driving east on the New Jersey Turnpike, driving through the New Jersey Meadowlands, making a right, and suddenly seeing the entire tip of Wall Street standing right across the Hudson River like a set of the greatest looking building blocks you can imagine.

Within ten minutes, the ferry docked. I like walking onto the ferry at that very moment when the boat rocks a bit and I know that I have stepped off the land.

All of New York City stretched out to my left. I saw the George Washington Bridge in the distance, the Empire State Building, the Chrysler Building. The World Trade Center once stood at the tip of Manhattan like two, great sentries standing watch over the city. The Statue of Liberty stood to my right. Her index finger alone is eight feet long. On the tablet held in her arm is a single inscription, a date: July 4, 1776.

I arrived too early for my lunch with Barbara, so I decided to visit St. Paul's Chapel, the oldest public building in continuous use in the city. Its construction was complete in 1766. The church's information packet proudly stated, "George Washington worshiped here on Inauguration Day, April 30, 1789, and attended services at St. Paul's during the two years New York City was the country's capital."

So there I was, with the ghost of Washington and the shadow of the Statue of Liberty, and soon to be sitting in a Chinese restaurant with my friend from the *Wall Street Journal*.

The first time I met Barbara was over the phone in 1984 when she called to say that the newspaper was accepting an essay I had sent in about the importance of reading to children. I was completing course work at Columbia University, and I remember working with Barbara over the pay phone in the administration building, as she made some editorial suggestions.

I was excited about being published in one of the greatest papers in the history of the United States. This was the first time any prose of mine was published.

Twenty-seven years later, I've been blessed with books, essays, and poems printed by major newspapers and publishing houses in the country, and now that I look back, I realize it was not the "corporations" that impressed me so much: it was the people: Mindy, my editor at Viking; John, my editor at HarperCollins; Virginia at Macmillan; Bob at Doubleday; Paul, Sandra, Dorothy—all people who toiled at the publication of words, who believed in a certain quality in a sentence, who considered the worth of ideas as a valid way to make a living.

Our country has been built upon the foundation of the ideas and words in the United States Constitution, in the Bill of Rights, in the Federalist Papers. We built our spiritual lives around ideas and holy books.

I have said to Barbara many, many times over the years how privileged she is to work with ideas that are read the next day by millions of people, and how, because of her intellect and splendid nature, she has influenced, for the good, countless people as they struggle in their offices, at their ranches, in their factories, in their homes, with daily issues that determine the value of a dollar and the value of human beings at work in a nation crying out for purposeful stability.

William Shakespeare wrote in his cherished play *Hamlet*, "What a piece of work is a man! How noble in reason! How infinite in faculty!...In apprehension how like a god!"

When I rode the ferry back to New Jersey, as the city leaned forward just a bit, trying to keep its hold on me, another ferry was on its way in to New York. A man stood on the deck. He waved, and I waved back. What a piece of work is a man.

We the People of the United States, in Order to form a more perfect Union, establish Justice, insure domestic Tranquility, provide for the common defence, promote the general Welfare, and secure the Blessings of Liberty to ourselves and our Posterity, do ordain and establish this Constitution for the United States of America.

We the people…We the people.

MAY 25

We all have our own life to pursue,
our own kind of dream to be weaving…
And we all have the power to make wishes come true,
as long as we keep believing.

—Louisa May Alcott

Before my father's stroke, he wove wide, beautiful, Aztec-like, Mexican-like wall hangings. In 1929, he built a weaving loom the size of a piano, made from oak and his imagination.

The loom sits in the living room, before the large front window. No one in my family ever had trouble finding a gift for my father: skeins of wool. For many years he wove mohair scarves, threading the wool back and forth hundreds of times with his weaving shuttle. He created regular, even designs that demanded precise calculations. He did the calculations in his head, and memorized each numbered execution.

Click clack. Click clack. I can still hear the machine in motion as my father pushes the foot pedal he designed that keeps the loom in action.

Often, when I visited him, one of the first things he'd say was, "Did you see my newest weaving?"

My father often took me to the loom or to his office and unfurled a four-foot cloth, good for hanging, or for using as a fancy throw rug, surely something unique, created by his hands.

When I visit, if I am alone with my mother, she will ask sometimes if I want to read one of her latest poems. My mother is one of the most distinguished American poets. I pick up a piece of paper and read a poem called "Writing."

> Black ink
> on the white field of the pages;
> Letters linked into a pattern
> into a chain of dark flowerets.
> What does it mean in the end?
>
> No more than the scrawl of the spider
> at work on its netting;
> No more than the zig-zags of the waterbug
> racing over the skin of the pond.
>
> Yet, over and under the lines
> one hears a measured living breath
> Easing itself into a kind of music
> and the sound lingers
> and the text sings.

I know the joy of the craftsmen displaying their wares. My father the weaver: "Here is a scarf." My mother the poet: "This is what I have written this afternoon."

There are three pears in a wood bowl on my kitchen table.

They are solid, fresh, the color of wet sand. I like to eat a pear in the afternoon when I am thirsty and a little hungry. I bite into the side of the pear and suck the juice. Sweet pear. Beautiful pear. Where did this pear come from? Who planted the tree? What is the name of the farm? What is the name of the man or the woman who pruned the trees and harvested the fruit?

When I was a child, I met Antoine. I was with my parents visiting friends, and they introduced us to Antoine. He was tall, like a grandfather clock. His beard hung like fleece from his smooth face. He was Russian and spoke little English.

While my mother and father spoke with their friends about music and books, Antoine, who looked bored, waved me over to his lap and then tugged on his beard a bit, inviting me to do the same. I pulled his beard, and when I did, his face smiled. When I pulled a second time, he frowned. Pull. Smile. Pull. Frown. We laughed and laughed. He then gently placed me on the floor, extended his hand, and brought me to his room. On his night table were bits of shavings and wood, a little hammer, a small saw, and loose string. Antoine reached across his table and picked up a toy. He had carved a little clown. The clown's arms were raised over its head and held onto a string extended between two pieces of wood, which were fastened together with a small brace.

If someone squeezed the little pieces of wood, the clown popped up as if it were doing an acrobatic movement over a high wire. When I saw the clown swing over the rope, I clapped. Antoine smiled and proffered the toy in my direction. He showed me how to work the stick, and then I too made the clown dance and wiggle over the string again and again. When I finished, I lifted the toy back to Antoine, but in the universal language, he smiled, and he pushed the toy back into my hands.

Who made the chair where I sit as I write? Who cut the glass for the windows in this house? I'd like to thank the people who built my car, glued my lamp shade, painted the lawnmower, and picked the red watermelon in the refrigerator. Who built the refrigerator?

Have we lost a sense of gratitude in our product-driven world? Do we no longer care who bakes our bread?

As my mother wrote in her poem: "One hears a measured living breath." How nice to know it is *her* voice in the poems that I read. I like knowing the weaving draped on the living room chair was created by the hands of my father. And no toy has matched for me the wooden, dancing clown that the old Russian made in his little room of shavings and dreams.

We can more fully divine the universe if we know the name of the creator.

MAY 27

Once in his life, every man is entitled to fall madly in love with a gorgeous redhead.

—Lucille Ball

I have been writing these little essays for the past twenty-seven years. When our children were small, they would chuckle and say at the dinner table, "Dad, are you going to write an essay about Karen learning how to ride a bike today?" Or, "Dad, write a story about how David won the soapbox derby at the Cub Scouts this week." Or, "Dad, write about how Michael got smacked in the head with a boomerang."

As the children grew older, they were less and less inclined to like seeing themselves in print, although Karen was delighted to see her name in *Good Housekeeping*, and Michael got a kick out of being in *Reader's Digest*, and David was amazed when he and his favorite stuffed animal ended up in the *New York Post*.

Often, when I give a talk somewhere in the country, someone will step up to me at the end of the presentation and ask, "How's Karen doing?" And I am amazed that this stranger knows about Karen. "But, Mr. De Vinck, you write about her all the time. I feel as if I know her."

Words printed in a newspaper or in a book have the ability to hold people together. I am still startled when I receive a letter from Africa about a book I wrote, or an e-mail from Poland about one of my essays.

Now our oldest, David, has moved out. He is in his fourth year in medical school. Karen has also moved on, working as a retail manager, and in love with a bright, wise young man. And Michael is in his third year of college, living with his friends in a house they all rented.

So some of the best characters for my essays have all grown up. Where does a writer go from here? Fiction, which I write. Poetry, which I have always written. But then there is always the memory, which brings me to Katie.

When I think of Katie, I smile and take great delight in her existence. Her mother, Linda, and father, Greg, were our friends long before Katie was born.

Katie has European-beautiful red hair. She has movie-star freckles. She is tall and lithe. Ever since I've known Katie, she loved to perform. There isn't a photograph or a videotape of Katie where she isn't dancing, joking, smiling, singing. I have seen this lovely child perform in high school band competitions, seen her running through her house with her brother and sister in their Christmas pajamas. Katie swam with our children, attended church with us, and celebrated most holidays with our two families.

We hear too much about tragedy in the newspapers. We are given pictures of violence and ugliness in the evening police dramas. How many times do we hear about the lost generation, or about youth being wasted on the young, or about young people these days not being contributors.

Today, Katie is twenty-six. She completed her college degree with honors in the field of speech pathology and is employed in a hospital. She tells us how good it is to help people to speak again after a stroke or accident.

When she was a little girl, Katie rushed up to me during one of our backyard barbecues and said with exuberance, "Why don't you write about me?" And then she ran off and performed jumping and running routines in step with the music on a cassette. So, I finally write about Katie.

May she continue to have the independence of Katherine Hepburn, the compassion of Florence Nightingale, the allure of Cleopatra, and the humor of Lucille Ball, all strong women who shared one thing for sure with Katie: red hair.

JUNE 2

The best and most beautiful things in the world cannot be seen or even touched. They must be felt within the heart.

—Helen Keller

"Superman! I think Lois Lane is locked in that steel vault!"

"Stand back, Jimmy. I'll take a look!"

The mighty man with X-ray vision places his hands on his waist, concentrates with his drilling eyes—and there, sure enough, deep inside the vault, he sees poor Lois tied to a chair, struggling. And, of course, Superman breaks through the vault as if it were JELL-O and rescues the grateful Lois Lane.

I once had X-ray vision. I could see through walls and watch my grandmother read the paper in the kitchen. If I held my hands across my eyes, I could see my brother's goofy face on the other side.

Actually, when I was a boy, my vision was my only true power over the world. All my brothers and sisters and both my parents wore glasses, but each time I had to go to the eye doctor, I was always able to read the small E no matter where it stood on the white chart hanging from the wall. I pretended that I had super-vision.

Last spring I was sitting in the garden in the full sun, reading the newspaper. It was the time of the year when the air is warm and then suddenly cool again. I felt a bit uncomfortable, so I collected the paper, stepped inside the house, sat on the living room couch, unfurled my paper, and began to read once again. I couldn't make out some of the words, so I clicked on a light. The words were still blurry. I complained aloud that the lamp was useless, that the paper company was using cheaper and cheaper ink.

The next day, and for the next month, I enjoyed my books and papers out on the deck in the full sun. Whenever it rained or clouded up, I'd try and sit in the house and read, but again found that the silly lamps were useless. I did not know that I needed glasses. Superman never needs glasses—only, of course, as part of his disguise.

When the eye doctor first asked me to read the chart filled with the letter E in all sorts of positions and sizes, I almost placed my hands on my waist and said, "No problem, Lois." But the more I looked, and the more I squinted, the more I realized either there was some kryptonite hidden in the room, or I was growing older.

A few weeks later I stood at a podium at a college in Illinois about to begin my presentation. When I reached into my jacket for my new glasses, they weren't there. They were abandoned, perhaps purposely, on the kitchen table back in New Jersey. When I jokingly said to the audience that I forgot my reading glasses, a woman in the front row pulled a black pair from her purse, stepped up to the stage, and extended her hand. But Superman doesn't need glasses, Lois.

I made my presentation, successfully read selections from my books, and thanked the audience. When I tried to return the glasses to the woman in the front row, she waved me on, saying, "Oh, they are just cheap pharmacy glasses. Keep them."

I use my cheap pharmacy glasses here at my desk where I write because, with their black rims, I look like Clark Kent. When I am in public, I wear my sleek, rimless, deluxe, crystal-powered, X-ray spectacles, and soar about the crowds faster than a speeding bullet, walk with more power than a locomotive, and leap tall buildings in a single bound.

My brother was blind. He never saw a squirrel, sailboats, a Yankees game, a painting by Memling, or a mountain. My brother never saw a ballet, or a cactus, or an ice-cream cone, or the Grand Canyon, or crayons.

No one knows for sure when glasses were invented. Around 1287, Italian paintings, for the first time, depicted people holding or wearing spectacles, so it is assumed that they were first created in Italy. In those earlier days, only noblemen or scholars wore glasses.

I am no nobleman, nor scholar. I am not even, in the end, Superman.

I'd often pick daffodils for my disabled brother and place them in a vase beside his bed. Perhaps I thought being in the proximity of beauty might, by some sort of osmosis, bring him pleasure. What we do not see can reveal hidden secrets. There are daffodils beside you.

Hawks can see a mouse from as high as one mile. The deeper a fish lives in the ocean, the bigger its eyes are. The natural world trains itself to enhance its vision for survival.

The first time I saw an elephant at the zoo, I staggered backward. How could something so large, and so wrinkled, and so powerful extend its long trunk and pick out a peanut from my sister's hand? You would almost have to see an elephant yourself in order to believe of its existence.

"Superman! The cat's locked in the basement!"

I'd stand before the door, stare hard, and say to my little sister, "Tiger Lilly is all right. Open the door." And my sister would open the door, and Tiger Lilly would step out like a triumphant queen in her fur coat.

But now the earth spins around in the darkness. We all seek power, which is nothing more than a unique commodity that others do not possess: authority, wealth, fame, strength. Being a middle child, being a man beyond middle age, living in the twenty-first century—these place a unique burden on the sense of self. I close my eyes and imagine spring. I close my eyes and remember swimming at the seashore when I was six. Close your eyes, and what do you see?

Helen Keller wrote, "The best and most beautiful things in the world cannot be seen or even touched. They must be felt within the heart."

Elephants. Superman. My brother. Daffodils. The Grand Canyon. Hawks. All, all is nothing without the divine soul of man closing his eyes, pointing, and saying with clarity, "I see. I see. Let no one doubt that I see."

JUNE 7

"The sky is falling! The sky is falling!"

—Chicken Little

Things fall from heaven or from oak trees. A novelist might describe the floating, soft descent of flowers, millions of flowers, landing on the grass and leaves, and call the event an accumulation of snow, when in the end it is the imagination replacing grief or loneliness. What better way to overcome sorrow than with a blizzard of chrysanthemums and roses?

In William Golding's novel *The Lord of the Flies*, the wild boys discover a corpse entangled in ropes and a torn parachute. The children believe that they have found a beast or devil, some monster that they have to fear and placate with sacrifices and loathing, when in reality what they have discovered is a dead man, a British pilot, a victim of war, something the children cannot understand.

Holy is the innocence that is not placed in the face of death in the context of old age.

When I was a boy, I liked to catch "helicopter seeds" as they whirled and whirled down from the maple trees. How much I liked splitting a seed open a bit, placing it on my nose, and proclaiming that I was Pinocchio!

Today I still like catching maple seeds. I like standing in the middle of a storm, and tilting my head back, and letting the water splash against my face. I like to catch snowflakes on my tongue. I like to fill the bird feeder and watch the cardinals and blue jays float down from the sky, and peck and call out in the joy of their discovery.

I am sorry that we no longer toss rice in the air at weddings. Remember the feel of the hard grain in our hands as we waited for the bride and groom to exit from the church? Remember the great fun it was to release the white rice from our hands and watch the sudden blizzard of luck shower down upon the couple in near slow motion, bouncing off the bride's veil, sticking to the groom's hair, as they both laughed and laughed?

We are pelted with hail. Violent winds destroy cities and towns. "The sky is falling! The sky is falling!" cries Chicken Little.

Dew descends like bits of diamond on the blades of grass as we sleep.

What is our lasting joy? What place does the sun have in our dreams? Or the moon? They both fall into the horizon, the great clock, the gears of our lives turning and turning as we are under the barrage of things that befall upon us.

What is our fate? What place do we call our destiny?

Last night, after I stopped writing, I stood up from my desk and walked to the French door to my right that leads out to the deck. I have a small thermometer on one window, and I wanted to check the temperature, which I do each night for no reason except, perhaps, to maintain a sense of order.

Sixty-six degrees. A cool night. I looked out into the darkness, and just beyond the soft, dim light from my desk lamp, I saw an object on the deck. I walked to the kitchen, found the flashlight, and then walked outside.

I flicked on the flashlight. Its yellow beam jiggled against the brown deck floor. I walked to what I thought was a large leaf. It was a young squirrel, sprawled out on the hard wood, blood oozing from its mouth. The animal was dead, having fallen out of its nest of leaves and dry grass perched high above the house.

I looked at the small, thin tail, the plump legs and belly. A gray squirrel, silk squirrel, swollen with death despite its sharp claws and luminous eyes.

What descends as a veil upon our lives each day? Yes, death. Of course, death. The endgame. Some might fear the lodging of the grave, fear the strife that comes with age, and fear the dwindling, waking days. A squirrel falls from its nest, and no one hears it smashing against the hard wood deck.

I do not know the landscape of heaven. Maybe in heaven it snows chrysanthemums. Maybe we are given a flashlight to find our way in the dark. I want to calculate the temperature in heaven, especially in the late evening. To me, heaven does not have ashes and hailstorms. Heaven is a place where you are invited to catch maple seeds twirling down on a July afternoon just before you go out for an ice-cream cone.

In my heaven, it rains rice and not dead pilots and little squirrels. I would be a happy gypsy in heaven, with my little family in a caravan, pots clanging against the sides of our wagons, coming in for the evening supper and a dance at the great fire.

We might not know the full triumph of heaven in our time, but such victory is always at hand, perhaps just beyond our reach, but there just the same, as we lean out the window and catch the falling roses and floating chrysanthemums.

JUNE 13

Home is the place where, when you have to go there,
they have to take you in.

—Robert Frost

I have lived in two houses: the house of my parents for twenty-six years, and now the house Roe and I bought thirty-four years ago. It is widely understood that Americans change their homes every seven years. When I tell my friends that my parents bought their home in 1948, and that they are both still living, people react as if I just said I know about this hidden place called Shangri La.

My father was born the year Titanic sank. My mother was born the year Yankee Stadium was built. I know that my father is home this afternoon sitting at his chair reading, perhaps, the history of China, and my mother is at her desk, writing her newest poem or reading *The New Yorker* magazine. My parents are healthy, intellectually acute, and actively involved in the national dialogue. My mother's pea soup was on the stove this past weekend.

In his famous poem "The Death of the Hired Man," Robert Frost wrote, "Home is the place where, when you have to go there, they have to take you in." For me, home is the place where the windows rattle and I am not afraid.

During a strong storm, the large windows in our old house would shake and whistle when I was a boy. Sometimes there was a low moan emanating from the poorly insulated front door, a siren sound, which sometimes combined with the rattle and bang of the iron radiators. But I, sitting next to my father as he read aloud, or cutting daffodil stems with my mother, felt safe, even as the wind and then the rain pounded against the house. Lightning illuminated the dimly lit rooms. Thunder rolled down, it seemed, from the dark rooms of the attic. But I was filled with peace and confidence. We liked to eat ice cream in a thunderstorm.

Now it is late spring, but I am told that I am already in the fall season of my "autobiography," having lived the first two quarters of my life.

This past month, the squirrels rebuilt their nests in the oak trees in the backyard. At the lake, the ducks arranged twigs and grass for their fresh eggs. The black bears in the northern part of the state have roused themselves, poked out their heads, and inhaled the new air and the solid evidence that, after their long slumber, they are still home. This is what we seek in our lives: the certitude that we have found our place, our home, even if we are, at times, in a reverie or in a deep sleep.

This is the season when children graduate from college, when weddings rings are traditionally exchanged, when the real estate market begins to boom once again. We are a people in the business of trying to recreate our homes. The greatest mission in our lives is to find our place. Where do we fit in? Where do we hang our coats in the evening? From what window do we gaze out in the middle of the night and feel safe?

In 1977, Roe and I bought our house: a two-bedroom, one-room-deep, white colonial with black shutters. As we were unloading our clothes, a dinette set, and my college refrigerator from the smallest U-Haul trailer the company rented, I walked to the front right corner of the yard and gazed up to our new home. My mother and my new wife were in the house opening boxes, hanging curtains, and as I looked at the front door and small windows, I asked myself, "I wonder what will happen here?"

For thirty-four years, I have stood at that corner and catalogued the chapters of a small family coming and going: the birth of three children, the death of a gold fish, thirty-four Christmas trees, three couches, birthday parties, proms, the phone ringing with news that a grandmother died in Belgium.

I step out of the house sometimes in the evening and stand at the same corner and look to the windows with the yellow lights pouring onto the grass like slabs of honey, and I know that Roe is sitting on the couch reading. The children are all adults and gone. The cat is dead, and yet there it is: home, the place where my wife tells me she loves me, the place where the walls hold pictures of the children when they *were* children, the place where the windows rattle and I am not afraid.

Part of the burdens of being an adult is accepting that we live with grief and sorrow. Our children are injured. Our parents die. We lose our jobs, perhaps divorce, mourn the loss of childhood, or regret a missed opportunity. When we are discouraged or filled with hopelessness, our minds spin in search of solace. What we discover are precious memories: times when we felt good, times when the summer lake was cool and soothing, days when a sister read aloud from the poetry of Carl Sandburg, an afternoon when a mother poured pea soup into the lunch bowl that sat, with a large, silver spoon, on the kitchen table before us—a witch's brew with curling steam.

I carry with me everywhere I go the key to my parents' house. I still have access to the home of my childhood, like Alice peeking through the tiny door where the White Rabbit disappeared into Wonderland.

One of my favorite books is *The Brothers Karamazov*, and in that book Dostoevsky wrote:

> From the house of my childhood I have brought nothing but precious memories, for there are no memories more precious than those of early childhood in one's first home. And that is almost always so if there is any love and harmony in the family at all. Indeed, precious memories may remain even of a bad home, if only the heart knows how to find what is precious.

We seek what is precious each day in our burdensome routines, and in the memories of what it was like to be young and delighted that the Good Humor ice-cream truck was only a few jingle bells away down the block.

No matter what pitch we are thrown in life, no matter how fast we stretch to reach first base, no matter how loudly the crowd roars or boos, we are always rushing to turn third base, trying to get back home.

I can still taste, no matter where I am, my mother's hot pea soup.

JUNE 19

I am but summer to your heart, and not the full four seasons of the year.

—Edna St. Vincent Millay

At the edge of summer, we find shells and seaglass strewn along the beach sand. Perhaps there is the anticipation of the roar at Yankee Stadium blasting from the apartment television, or the hope for the first open hydrant. Perhaps we listen, once again, for the pleasure of the clacking sound of the invisible tractor just over the hillside, plowing the earth.

For me, summer is the evidence that there is far more to a human being than the gloom of winter or the harsh cold that can consume a weary heart.

In the middle of February, when the ground is frozen and the sky, a slate gray, is bloated with coming snow, I often think of McPhee Bay. I do not know why we call it McPhee Bay. It is hardly a bay, more a small inlet off to the side of the Madawaska, a wide, slow-moving river five hundred miles north of my New Jersey home, lapping the sandy shore by our small Canadian cabin.

Every summer since I was a boy, my family and I have

made the trip to the Madawaska. For the past twenty years, we've had a motorboat.

As a boy, I was happy to float on a rubber raft, or borrow the neighbor's canoe, and paddle through the water lilies and pretend that I was Davey Crockett. As I grew older, I longed to own a powerboat and skim across the blue water with a girl at my side.

Canada in July is like a freshly painted masterpiece: Limoges-blue skies, pine-green mountains, all illuminated with the light of the honey sun that seems to highlight the best part of the season and ourselves.

One summer afternoon, Roe, our three children, David, Karen and Michael, my sister Maria, my brother-in-law Peter, and their two children, Sarah and Christopher, all set off in the motorboat and headed for McPhee Bay. We had no lunch, no skis, no plan, just a sudden summer choice to zoom off the beach, turn right, and splash our way through the blue water.

As Peter drove, the Canadian air rushed through his hair as he adjusted his sunglasses. The girls sat in the bow rider, laughing each time the boat rose and dropped into the willing river. I sat in the back with my nephew and sons as we dragged our hands in the water, teasing each other about our arm muscles. We all agreed that mine were the most invisible.

Suddenly Michael pointed to the left and shouted, "Loons!" Peter swung the boat in a sudden arc as he cut back the engine, and we slowly moved in the direction of the two loons and their three chicks. Only because the chicks were helpless were we allowed to slide so close to the family.

"Look how cute the babies are," Karen said.

We all watched the large loons circle around as they protected their young. The little ones hopped onto the backs of the parents, or paddled around in the water, looking like bathtub windup toys.

"Okay," Peter said. "Let's go." He pushed the advance lever

down, and the motorboat engine eagerly roared back to life. "McPhee Bay to the left," Peter pointed. Everyone looked out and we all pointed, as though we were ancient mariners on a mission, perhaps trying to evade the shadow of the albatross.

When we skimmed into the bay, which was about the size of a mall parking lot, Peter cut the engine, and the boat slowly slid to silence and stopped. We all looked at the summer trees that lined the small bay, and took notice of a heron that flew like a loose, Japanese kite over the water and disappeared beyond the distant hill.

Suddenly: "Last one in is a rotten egg!" Sarah yelled, and five teenagers jumped into the water with their uncle, aunt, and mother. I sniveled a bit, saying that someone had to stay with the boat and the water looked cold.

I watched Roe swim with our three children as they splashed her and she splashed them back. Peter swam under the water and popped up behind Sarah and tickled her. Maria laughed. David, Michael, and Chris began a game of tag, using the boat ladder as home base as they swam under and around the boat like dolphins. I could hear the echo of their laughter bouncing off the surrounding hills.

As I sat in the boat, watching my own loon family bobbing on the surface of McPhee Bay, I thought of the Samuel Coleridge quote: "A spring of love gushed from my heart, and I blessed them unaware." I struggle during the year to be a good husband, father, brother, and brother-in-law.

At night in our cabin, I look out the window and acknowledge the magic of the fruitful moon illuminating the still river. I listen to the distant loons crying out in the blue darkness.

During the regular routines of my life, smeared with the ink of disheartening newspaper headlines, in the middle of February when the bills seem crushing and the yard is constricted in cold and ice, when I feel a bit drained and not such a good husband or father or brother or brother-in-law, I think of McPhee Bay and the summer loons splashing each other, swimming under the boat like summer Poseidons, and I accept, as the poet Edna St. Vincent Millay wrote, that "I am but summer to your heart, and not the full four seasons of the year."

Oh, if we could be our summer selves 365 days of the year.

Summer

It will not always be summer: build barns.

—Hesiod

JUNE 21

Summer afternoon—summer afternoon;
to me those have always been the two most
beautiful words in the English language.

—Henry James

Today is the first day of summer. The earth's axis is pointing toward the sun, giving us the highest exposure to the sun's heat, and my grandmother is pointing her finger at the ice-cream truck that is parked at the edge of the driveway.

Deep inside my New Jersey summers when I was a boy, I would beat a path to the ice-cream truck. There was no better way to spend ten minutes than to sit on the curb with my sister as we ate our Good Humor Toasted Almond Ice-Cream Bars and our Rocket Pops.

Summers long ago meant hunting for salamanders in the wet marsh, playing Red Light/Green Light on the front lawn, turning maple leaves into dollars, building huts with cut grass and bent sticks from the mock-orange bushes. We conquered the humidity as we chased each other with the spurting hose or with loaded water guns and with days down at the public pool where the water jiggled blue and clear—my sister was such a baby wearing her nose clip.

Huckleberry Finn couldn't have been happier if he chose to ride side by side with me in 1963 as we'd pedal our bikes, the ones with fenders and plastic, colored streamers dangling from our handlebars. I'd show Huck how to eat Lik-M-Aid or how to drink Nik-L-Nips, those inch-high wax bottles of sugar juice.

The men at the firehouse always seemed willing to give out free cans of cold soda in the summer, and the Erie Lackawanna made it easy to place a penny on the railroad track. I'd show it to my brother that night and trade my squashed penny for his Mickey Mantle baseball card.

Summer once belonged to children, and was the place where school buildings were abandoned, and fireflies were caught in glass jars with holes in the lids; the place where teenagers could kiss or go skinny dipping, and no one would know except your best friend Billy or the wide, all-seeing moon, and Jenny laughed as her wet hair dripped down her back, and we'd buy a slice of pizza to embellish our alibis.

One summer Jim Bouton, the famous Yankee player, came to Allendale to pitch for the Merchants in the Metro League. I bought Cracker Jack and rode my bike over to the ball field. "I've never seen a Yankee in person," I said to my friends as I saw Bouton's famous smile.

My last summer as a boy, I was a lifeguard. Karen was my girlfriend at the time. She was blonde and smart, and had volunteered for "We Care," a summer program for inner city children. She brought the children to the pool where I worked and played ring-around-the-rosy with them in the water. When the children shouted, "We all fall down!" Karen and twenty little boys and girls all disappeared under the water, and when they popped up, the children gasped and wiped the water from their eyes. Karen would laugh, turn to me, and wave. The children often asked if I would blow my whistle and I did, and all the children laughed, and the sun laughed, and it was August.

The poet Archibald MacLeish wrote, "Summer is drawn blinds in Louisiana, long winds in Wyoming, shade of elms in New England." For me, eternal summer is the jingle of the Good Humor truck, a sister shouting "Red Light!"—the splash of water, the sound of the lifeguard's whistle.

Happy the boy who built a summer raft with popsicle sticks. Happy the man who still remembers how.

JUNE 22

"My advice to you is not to inquire why or whither, but just enjoy the ice cream while it's on your plate."

—Thornton Wilder

Yesterday, while gently submerging the roots of young tomato plants in my small backyard, I heard in the distance the jingling of a children's song. It was the ice-cream truck. I hadn't heard the ice-cream truck in our neighborhood for ten years.

Roe was at work. The neighborhood was empty. I looked at my soiled hands, and then turned to see the truck drive around the bend, and I knew that within a few minutes, it would return as it made its way around our court.

Each summer when I was a child, my sister and I were given 25 cents to buy ice cream down at the Allendale Municipal Pool, where the Good Humor truck stopped each afternoon. I liked the ice-cream man's bow tie. I liked his white uniform. I liked listening to the solid click of the thick, little door in the back of the truck as it was opened and closed. I liked looking at the menu pictures posted on the side of the truck: chocolate éclairs, Good Humor Toasted Almond Ice-Cream Bars, red-and-orange Popsicles, vanilla cones, ice-cream sandwiches.

The Roman emperor Nero, more than 2,000 years ago, ate snow harvested from the mountains, which was mixed with fruit and nectar. George Washington served ice cream to his friends.

I returned to my tomato plants. I am sixty years old.

For many years, every Monday night my father returned from work with a half gallon of ice cream, always the inexpensive brand and always Neapolitan: chocolate, vanilla, and strawberry in one container. I would trade my strawberry portion with my sister for her chocolate portion.

Jingle! Jingle! Jingle!

I looked up from the tomato plants. I knew my knees were stained with soil.

Jingle! Jingle! Jingle!

I quickly stood, looked around, saw that I was still alone, and so ran to the house and up into the kitchen like a ten-year-old boy, grabbed my wallet, and rushed out the door to the street. As I stood at the edge of the lawn, I could see the ice-cream truck making the turn around the neighbor's hedge.

President Ronald Reagan declared in 1984 that July would be, from then on, National Ice-Cream Month. I've read that the total U.S. sales of ice cream is $23 billion yearly.

I waved my hand and flagged down the ice-cream truck. It pulled up to my side, and I was quickly greeted by a man with a smile and a question: "What can I get you?"

I wanted to ask if he could return my father on Monday nights, or find my sister down at the swimming pool. Instead, I asked for a chocolate éclair.

The writer Thornton Wilder wrote in his famous play *The Skin of Our Teeth*: "My advice to you is not to inquire why or whither, but just enjoy your ice cream while it's on your plate— that's my philosophy."

Summer is a time to fool ourselves, a time to believe that tomato plants can distract us from sorrow or loneliness, a time to pursue little bells and ice-cream sticks in our attempt to slide in a moment's pleasure during our listless days of doubt.

Yes. Seize the day. The ice cream is delicious and cold. That's my philosophy.

JULY 1

The only emperor is the emperor of ice cream.

—Wallace Stevens

July is the month for watermelons and lemonade, barbeques and cold beer, but for me these coming weeks will always be identified as the season for ice cream.

I saw my grandfather only in the summer. He and my grandmother visited us from Belgium during June, July, and August, and it was his routine to escort me once a week to the Allendale Sweet Shoppe for an ice-cream sundae.

I was always half-afraid of my grandfather, and half-delighted: frightened because he was a demanding, retired general in the Belgian Army, and delighted because he held my hand when we crossed the busy Franklin Turnpike.

I liked scrambling up on the Norman Rockwell stool in the ice-cream parlor and submitting my adult-like order: "A chocolate sundae with whipped cream and a cherry, please." My grandfather never ordered anything for himself. He just sat next to me on his stool, swiveling back and forth a bit. I remember the aroma of his shaving lotion and the image of his wrinkled hand as he pulled out two crisp dollar bills from his brown wallet.

Some people eat ice cream with their teeth, biting into a cone. Other people use a spoon like a magic stick, dipping into a cup of vanilla raspberry as if the ice cream would last forever.

Johnny, my best friend, ate ice cream with his lips. He would hold a white Dairy Queen cone in his hand and use his top lip to lop off a smooth wad of ice cream. I am a licker, rolling my tongue from the bottom of the cone to the top. Some people lick their ice-cream cones from side to side, rotating the cone as if it were a diamond for inspection.

Ice cream was expensive when I was a boy, growing up in a family of six children, so when my mother discovered an ice-cream mix, I thought that I had entered ice-cream paradise.

Somehow my mother created this smooth concoction using water and a blender, and then she poured the gooey invention into an ice tray. The next day my sisters and brothers and I gathered around her as she cut out small squares of what we called strawberry ice cream. It was cold, it tasted like strawberries, and it was easy for me to imagine that I was standing at a fancy ocean resort eating the dessert of the gods.

I liked how, when my father ate ice cream, he used his spoon like a gold miner, scraping the very last bit of chocolate from the bottom of the bowl, and extracting a last bit of flavor. My father is ninety-nine years old and he doesn't eat ice cream anymore. "Too cold."

Every Thursday afternoon I visit my father in the same house where I grew up. On my way to Allendale, I stop at Curly's Ice Cream in Riverdale on busy Route 23. It has been around for fifty years, run by the same family. I love Curly's chocolate ice-cream cones. When I lick from the bottom up, I close my eyes, and there is my father, scraping the last ice cream from his bowl with delight. There is Johnny, using his lips like a camel, nearly kissing the white, cold vanilla. And there is my mother, asking "Christopher, would you like another scoop of my homemade ice cream?"

When I open my eyes, I look at my own wrinkled hand and listen to the roar of traffic on the highway.

I am the ice-cream soldier holding my grandfather's hand in the hot, July afternoon.

"You scream, I scream, we all scream for ice cream!"

JULY 2

"We always returned to Paris."

—Ernest Hemingway

Summer is the season to save ourselves. If we are lucky enough, we have a week or two of vacation when time stops, the loons or the ocean waves lull us to sleep, and a book reminds us that there is a soul-self that needs to be rejuvenated.

In a used-book shop, I found Ernest Hemingway's bittersweet, posthumously published memoir, *A Moveable Feast*. This past month, as I sat during a number of afternoons on the beach of a Canadian lake, I pretended that I was the great writer, sipping café au lait in a warm and friendly café on the Place St-Michel in Paris.

It was a time between the two European wars. Hemingway was still in love with his first wife, Hadley. Between writing his great novels and betting at the Auteuil and the Enghien horse tracks, he entertained Gertrude Stein, F. Scott Fitzgerald, Ezra Pound, and Archibald MacLeish, all part of the group we call "expatriates," those writers and artists who, in the 1920s and 1930s, left America in search of the ephemeral muse and with a passion for a city we call Paris but, in reality, we call ourselves.

I found, for myself, a number of significant lines in Hemingway's book: "Write one true sentence, and then go on from there."

And this: "They say seeds of what we will do are in all of us." And this: "Everything good and bad left an emptiness when it stopped."

Hemingway was, perhaps, the happiest in his life during those years in Paris, when he and his wife had little money, lived in a small apartment, imagined the aroma of spring, and witnessed his talent emerging day by day. But in the end, the novelist strayed from all that was Paris and happy. "All things truly wicked start from an innocence," he wrote. "So you live day by day and enjoy what you have and do not worry. You lie and hate and it destroys you and every day is more dangerous, but you live day to day as in a war."

On our last night in Canada this summer, I dragged the canoe to the edge of the beach and slipped out, alone, to the middle of the lake to enjoy the sunset. My paddle cut into the still water, and with a simple flex of my shoulder and arm muscles, the canoe slid along as if on ice or slick oil. There was no sound.

Sunsets in Canada are distinctive, especially when the clouds layer themselves at the tip of the horizon, and the low, green hills begin to turn black. The sun sinks behind the hills and projects orange light under the low clouds, which creates a splash of light, a panorama of orange and yellow, and all seems held in an eighteenth-century landscape painting in celebration of all that is still, sudden, and beautiful.

As I waited for the sun to position itself, I happened to notice on the surface of the water a slight movement. Small ripples appeared from a small center in the water, from a small dot, from a small creature struggling in the water: a dragonfly. Any moment the insect would be eaten by a bass or catfish.

I quickly paddled my canoe parallel to the dragonfly, and then I slowly extended the paddle until the tip was under its four black legs and four soaking wings. I slowly lifted the paddle, lifted the drenched, struggling dragonfly into the canoe, and placed it on the empty seat.

As I watched the sun close the day, I checked on the dragonfly. At first it didn't move. Then it stood up on its legs. By the time the sun had gone behind the hills completely, the dragonfly was beating its four wings in the air until they were dry enough for flight.

The sky lit up in flames of orange and red as the dragonfly lifted itself from the canoe seat, hovered in the air before me, then began to fly higher and higher until I could no longer see it.

I am home now. The vacation is over. When Hemingway broke off with his wife he wrote, "Paris was never to be the same again although it was always Paris and you changed as it changed."

It turns out that we human beings understand love, truly, at the end of our lives. It is in looking back that we can assess the whole, remember the idea of love, create in our hearts a nostalgia for stillness and summers at the lake, and a time when the sunset was worthy of notice.

Hemingway was right. When you stop love, "you lie and hate and it destroys you and every day is more dangerous, but you live day to day as in a war."

There is, skimming across a Canadian lake, a lucky dragonfly, scooping up mosquitoes, hovering in the air, zipping to shore in search of a dry twig to perch on for the night.

We all struggle on the water's surface, in fear of being swallowed whole by the great fish. We do live a war within ourselves each day, but in the end, if we pay attention, believe in providence, dream, love, and return to our true selves now and again, we are rescued from death and loneliness.

We are not helpless creatures with our arms and legs spread out on the water's surface. We have the ability to remember the taste of honey and the voices of those we loved.

"We always returned to Paris," Hemingway wrote in the last page of his little book, "no matter who we were or how it was changed or with what difficulties, or ease, it could be reached."

We always return to vacations no matter how much we have changed, in order to remember the cold lake water against our skin as we rushed out from the dry beach.

We return to listen to the loons and the ocean and the stillness, as we know for sure that we will someday die, and we remember when we were young and very happy, and we recognize, in the beating of the dragonfly's wings, that we too will be saved.

JULY 3

When you finally go back to your old hometown, you find it wasn't the old home you missed but your childhood.

—Sam Ewing

I grew up in a small northern New Jersey town cut in two by the Erie Lackawanna Railroad. All my town really needed was the Mississippi River to run smack down the middle, and I, the new Huckleberry Finn, would have lashed together some pine logs, crept out of the house at midnight, and pushed off for Louisiana—or else hitched myself to a few stars and flung my way to the moon and never return.

But the best I had was the celery farm, known today as a nature preserve—a swamp, really, that seeped up from the glacier's retreat in the middle of New Jersey. It was there that my sisters and brothers and I opened our coats and pretended we were sailboats on ice, as the wind pushed us from one end of the frozen swamp to the other.

It was there I pretended that I was the Swamp Fox: Brigadier General Francis Marion, the famous American Revolutionary commander from South Carolina who foiled the British army again and again by disrupting their communications, attacking unsuspecting soldiers, and rescuing captured Revolutionary troops from the King's men. Each time General Marion carried out one of his raids, he eluded the British by disappearing into the tangled and secret swamps he knew so well.

If I could not be Huckleberry Finn, I could be the Swamp Fox. I raided my grandfather's vegetable garden, eluded the neighbor's dogs, in the spring pretended that the duck eggs I found were for my breakfast—and I'd run back into the swamp among the cattails and tall grass, and inhale summer like a boy about to turn into Hercules.

Then I heard the Beatles for the first time on my sister's turquoise, plastic radio, and I became Paul McCartney and a New Jersey teenager all at once.

Cousin Brucie pulled me off Huckleberry Finn's raft and introduced me to Herman's Hermits and the Lovin' Spoonful. I grew my hair in the shape of a bowl, read *Catcher in the Rye* in my high school English class, kissed a girl for the first time (Jenny—smart, pretty, artistic Jenny, who probably quickly discovered that I was more Huckleberry Finn than Paul Newman).

New Jersey was a great billboard set up behind the highway of my childhood. Like a plastic tiara, Palisades Amusement Park sat on the cliffs overlooking Manhattan. Anyone who ate at the Leaning Tower of Pizza on Route 17 in Ramsey could claim international status as a world connoisseur of fine dining. Dr. Zhivago froze on the drive-in movie screen. Long Beach Island was the place where Laura, a geeky high school clarinet player, was transformed to a bikini starlet right out of the James Bond movie *Thunderball*. I remember skiing at Campgaw Mountain in Mahwah, grabbing a hamburger at the Fireplace Restaurant, buying dessert at Jahn's Ice-Cream Parlor in Fair Lawn.

But somehow, thankfully, most teenagers emerge from their Bozo the Clown personas and stumble into adulthood.

How nice to land safely as a young man into the poetry of New Jersey's famous writers: Walt Whitman and William Carlos Willams. Sussex County is a great place to meet a young woman and fall in love, dine with her at the Meadows Restaurant, hike with her at High Point State Park.

When our children began to grow, Roe and I drove them to the Morristown Museum, the Twin Lighthouse at Sandy Hook, Space Farms, Van Saun Park. We hiked at Hacklebarney State Park, picked pumpkins in Morris County, cut down Christmas trees in Warren County, and sent all three children to Rutgers University.

The first recorded baseball game was played in Hoboken. New Jersey has the most diners in the world. The honeybee is our state insect; the goldfinch is our state bird.

The Pulitzer Prize–winning journalist John Ed Pearce, who died in 2006, once wrote, "Home is a place you grow up wanting to leave, and grow old wanting to get back to."

Many, many years ago, I was ready to hop onto my raft and sail away from New Jersey, but the adage is true in many ways: we grow where we are planted.

I've been to Paris, walked through the side streets of Rome, flew to England. I've been to nearly every state in the Union, but I...well...I just like finding my little place just beyond the Ramapo Mountains, near where the Lenni Lenape Indians lived, over there in New Jersey—a place where I go back to at the end of my travels, a land of stars, hundreds of towns glowing under the belly of the 747 as I descend into Newark Airport.

Washington really slept everywhere in New Jersey. Some say that we have the Jersey Devil lurking around the Pine Barrens. Some people call New Jersey the Garden State. I call New Jersey home, the place where the lighthouse is always lit.

JULY 4

There are those, I know, who will say that the liberation of humanity, the freedom of man and mind, is nothing but a dream. They are right. It is the American dream.

—Archibald MacLeish

A few years ago, as I was flying home from the Midwest following a book tour I had just completed, I looked out the window as the jet began its slow descent over New Jersey, approaching Newark Airport. There, far below, I saw wide bursts of light: greens, yellows, reds. They were, of course, fireworks, for I was returning home on the Fourth of July, and flying over Warren, Morris, and Essex Counties.

Town after town was celebrating Independence Day with fireworks. The odd part was that these exploded in silence. Sitting in my seat in the jet I, of course, could not hear the booms and bangs, or the roar of the crowds in approval, but I could see the little fountains of light bursting up like Walt Disney mushrooms all over the state. Then I thought of my grandmother.

During World War II, Nazi SS troops banged on the door of my grandmother's house in Brussels, searching for my grandfather, an officer in the Belgian Army. He managed to escape, but was soon captured and sent to a Spanish prison.

My grandmother often spoke about how she and my mother fled Brussels and ended up in a small, French coastal city: Dunkirk. They witnessed the evacuation of thousands of Allied troops across the English Channel, and continued their escape to southern France, but, after four months, they returned to Brussels and endured the Third Reich's occupation for four years.

"Bombs always seemed to be falling," my grandmother said. She and my mother even remembered hearing the distant explosions from the Battle of the Bulge, the last attempt of the Nazi forces to overtake Europe, and the most horrific battle in the war, where over 19,000 American troops died.

One of the last summers my grandmother was with us here in New Jersey, I was sitting with her in the dining room playing gin rummy. It was the Fourth of July. For no reason, I began humming John Philip Sousa's "Stars and Stripes Forever," perhaps the most famous march in the world, recognized as the official march of the United States.

"Da, daa, da, da, daa, da, da, da, da, da, daa…"

As I hummed, my grandmother picked from the deck of cards, and then she began to quietly hum the march as well. I picked from the deck and began to whistle the tune. She picked her next card and began to hum louder. I looked at her. She looked at me. I started to hum even louder as I reached for the salt shaker and began pounding the table as if it was a drum accompanying my humming. She placed her cards on the table—"Gin!"—and then she grabbed the pepper shaker and banged the tune on the table along with the humming.

The two of us then gave our best impersonations of full Marine bands, belting out the grand march. We whistled, clapped, banged the salt and pepper shakers on the table, and, at the final crescendo, we ended together on the last, resounding note—and we both felt fine.

Then, suddenly, the first fireworks exploded over the Allendale baseball field: Boom! Boom! And my grandmother looked at me and said quietly, "I never liked fireworks. They sound so much like the bombs dropping during the war."

I asked her if she'd like to play another round of gin. "Yes," she said with a smile. As I dealt the cards, she looked out over her reading glasses and said, "Vive l'Amérique." And we both hummed "Stars and Stripes Forever" all over again.

All across New Jersey, all across the nation: Boom! Boom! Boom! Vive l'Amérique!

JULY 5

The people, yes.

—Carl Sandburg

Does anyone remember the way things used to be: when the artist Norman Rockwell sketched boys rushing off to fish; when you could pick up hitchhikers; when gas-station attendants wore white shirts and ties and gave away glasses with each full tank of gas?

Remember how we could go off to the woods, swimming hole, or train tracks, and pretend that we were Daniel Boone, Olympic stars, or hoboes, and rush home in the late afternoon for a glass of Kool-Aid? Remember when the Cracker Jack box had great prizes: alligator clickers, charms, jumping tin frogs?

There was once a thing called the Good Humor truck. Every child born before 1960 remembers the sound the door made closing after the ice-cream man reached in and pulled out a chocolate éclair or a Fudgsicle.

It is easy to dismiss our "modern" world and roll ourselves in a security blanket of nostalgia, pointing to better times when people were more polite and less afraid.

Don't believe everything you read in the newspapers or see on television. The accumulation of evidence about the state of the world is not neatly packaged and printed on paper, or projected on flat screens that illuminate our faces and lull us into a near-hypnotic trance of delusion and disgust. Goodness is not news. Compassion is not news. The triumph of our daily routines accrues no hero's welcome.

I was reminded of the grace of goodness that most of us have within ourselves while driving home with my mother and Roe from our annual two-week vacation in Canada. (My father didn't come with us that year.)

Just before mile marker 175 on Route 81 south, just twenty miles from Watertown, New York, my car developed engine trouble. The alternator light popped on. The check-engine light blinked frantically. The temperature gauge swung to the right, smack into the heart of the "hot" indicator. There was a gross, mechanical noise whining and clanking under the hood.

I quickly pulled into a U-turn road built for police and maintenance crews, pushed the gearshift into park, shut off the engine, opened the hood, and felt like Dorothy in the *Wizard of Oz* stuck in the middle of a poppy field ready to call out for help. Glinda the Good Witch didn't appear, but within four minutes, a New York state trooper pulled off the northbound lane of the highway, drove down the small U-turn road and stopped before us. I wanted to shout hooray! It was as though Roy Rogers or Zorro had come to my rescue.

He was a young man: dark hair, crew cut, sunglasses, smart uniform. He stepped out of his cruiser and, with great politeness and concern, asked if we were okay. I explained that my wife was on the cell phone with AAA, and that my mother was in the car doing fine.

The policeman was concerned about my mother and spoke with AAA himself, and once he was assured that the tow truck was coming, he said, "I'll swing by again in a few minutes just to make sure that you are okay and on your way." It was obvious that this man had a human interest in us and that he was not just "doing a job." He drove away and waved. I waved too.

Before the tow truck arrived, a park ranger stopped, asking if we needed help; a Good Samaritan in a van also stopped and asked if we needed a ride; and then the tow truck and its driver appeared.

This man was blond, well built, tall, confident. "Right there is your trouble," he said, as he pointed to two belts that looked like shredded snakes trapped within the guts of the engine. "It could be that the alternator seized and caused the belt to snap. Whatever happened, the one belt cut into the other and your fan stopped spinning, which caused your radiator to overheat."

I leaned over the engine, pretending I was as wise as Merlin when it came to auto mechanics, and said, "What do we do?"

Ten minutes later, Roe, my mother, our dog, and I were in a tow truck, riding to Watertown with our van behind us like a broken hippopotamus.

The tow truck driver spoke about his wife and children, about his work with the Special Olympics. I thanked him for his helping us. He said again and again, "I know what it is like to be stranded and people don't help you out." He was concerned about my mother, drove us to the Ramada Inn in Watertown first, so my mother would not be upset and she could settle in. Then he drove me and my car to the Mazda dealer in Watertown.

The mechanic, his name was Lou, seemed right from central casting. He looked like Nicholas Cage and was as kind and helpful as St. Christopher. "Could be the alternator, or just the belts. I can get you going by tomorrow morning." As we talked, we spoke about our lives a bit, about our children and jobs.

Who are we as a people? The state trooper's immediate arrival and his kindness? The tow truck driver's demeanor and grace? (We exchanged addresses and I sent him one of my books.) The mechanic who shook my hand warmly when I was about to drive out of the parking lot with my repaired automobile? Even the woman behind the desk at the Ramada Inn was concerned about our plight, rearranged some rooms, agreed right away to take the dog, even though there were "no pet" signs prominently displayed. "We'll make you as comfortable as possible."

Remember the old *Saturday Evening Post* magazine? Norman Rockwell, with his talent, could have illustrated the cover of this week's issue with a group portrait: a policeman, a tow truck operator, a mechanic, a Good Samaritan, and a hotel clerk, and he would have given us, with his brushes and paint, just the right angles, just the right texture, just the right colors and light to depict America.

JULY 6

There is only one real deprivation…and that is not to be able to give one's gifts to those one loves most.

—May Sarton

We have doubts about our worthiness, about our abilities, or about our place in life. Often those feelings of insecurity are washed away by mothers, fathers, husbands, and wives. Often, though, we need the objective eye of a friend to tell us what we need to hear at just the right moment.

I have been a writer for thirty-one years, and as anyone familiar with the creation of anything knows, there are doubts along the way. Can I write? Am I a fool to think that I can compete with the writers that I admire the most: William Carlos Williams? F. Scott Fitzgerald? Harper Lee?

Many years ago I became friends with the poet and novelist May Sarton. We met on the set of *Mister Rogers' Neighborhood*, both being Fred Rogers' guests on his grace-filled children's television program. Since that first meeting, May and I exchanged many, many letters, and she often invited me to visit her at her home in York, Maine. Her house overlooked the wide Atlantic Ocean.

During one visit, after dinner May said, "Chris, I'd like you to sit next to me on the couch and read aloud some of your poems."

May was well into her eighties, stooped, frail. She slowly walked to the living room couch, sat down, adjusted a lamp as I pulled out a folder of poems from my small, leather briefcase. We sat like two contented sea otters, satisfied with the fresh lobster dinner we had just eaten, and so I began to select various poems from my folder, and I read aloud. I held the papers close enough so that we could both read at the same time.

After each poem, May made a comment: "I like that one," or, "This word doesn't sound right here." I read my poems for about half an hour, and then May turned to me and said, "You are a writer."

As I drove home the next morning, I wanted to tell the toll collector on the New Hampshire highway that May Sarton thought that I was a writer. When I arrived home that evening, Roe asked me how my trip went. "May said that I am a writer."

A few weeks later, May said to me on the phone, "Remember, Chris, because you are my friend, I cannot lie to you. If I didn't like your work, I would have said so too."

We need in our lives people who tell us that we are on the right track. While people in our families give us, of course, confidence, a friend can give us confidence in a different way. We human beings are complicated. We need mothers, fathers, *and* we need friends to satisfy all the various elements of what it means to be who we are. A friend objectively reaches out with love and tells us that we are on the right track. A friend is a bridge between our lonely self and our true self.

JULY 7

"…deriving their just powers from the consent of the governed.…"
—The Declaration of Independence

We are a nation adrift. Core values have been abandoned in our corporate offices. The American flag hangs in shame to lawless, pre-emptive attacks that disregard the Constitution and the memory of American troops liberating Europe in the name of what was just.

We take our sustenance from the sweet milk of fantasy, believing power, money, and comfort take precedence over the hungry, the ignorant, the disabled—over a choked, coal-dusted planet.

Profit determines the appearance of our compassion and the resolve we promote in our fight against evil; in reality, evil defined according to selective convenience eventually destroys the decision maker.

I believe we need to be a people of tolerance, celebrating pluralism while, at the same time, celebrating the gracious, wide composition of what it means to be a human being. We need to redefine our national misfortunes, not the fight over abortion, not the misinterpretation of God's will, not the pretense of profit for the national good. We need, I believe, to redefine the tragedy of our cities, to redefine education, and to reestablish our good name in the international community, based on human rights both here at home and abroad.

We need a way to make our business and political transactions transparent, create an equal and fair distribution of the tax burden, reestablish our commitment to the separation of church and state, sever the grip insurance companies and lawyers hold on the fluid exchange of goods and services, and establish maximum rates on easily defined, basic goods: food, clothing, and shelter.

We need to reject career politicians, and the hubris of nationalism. We need the pin of common sense to bore through the armor plate of our arrogance.

Democracy is, by necessity, a sloppy system of governance that can bulge under the influence of conservatism and liberalism at the same time, but such democracy is threatened when corrupt order, rules, and law attempt to redefine the core values of a nation that were established upon the equal, inalienable rights of all its citizens to thrive under the protection of life, liberty, and the pursuit of happiness.

We are not at the cusp of victory on any frontier in our nation today. Science is stalled, the stock market is mistreated and manipulated daily, the value of work is diminished, equated with profit and not with a sense of vocation and loyalty.

Churches, synagogues, and mosques have abandoned the Gospels, the Torah, and the Qur'an.

I do believe we are a patient people, living our lives in the great waiting, convinced we know what we want, anxious for a presidential candidate who will honor us with a victory based on true representation *of* the people, *by* the people, and *for* the people.

Step away from money. Step away from lobbyists. Step away from polls, greed, and power. No one is fooling anyone anymore. We as a people understand advertising gimmicks and consultant ploys. We are not, at the moment, a proud people. We are in a state of national grief, mourning the death of soldiers, being appalled at the shameful display of public corruption both in Washington and on Wall Street, and avoiding the ever-widening wedge of discrimination.

Those in power take a few frightening words and sell them to people to make them afraid, expecting them to buy into a product or a policy that will make them feel a little less frightened and feel a little more secure. In reality, we do not like what is being sold, and we believe there is a better voice and a stable journey ahead, a universal conviction of goodness that is recognizable even under the onslaught of deception and manipulation.

Our government was conceived in the open light of the Constitution, and in the public battlefields at Lexington and Concord, Stony Point and Yorktown. Our history as a people was created under the vibrant red, white, and blue flag studded with stars, representing the transparent truth of goodness, integrity, and freedom.

We do not live in a clear, clean system any longer. We do not live in a country that was conceived by Washington and Jefferson. The victory of the American Revolution has been eroded, and the flag is not being used any longer as a national blanket, but as a cheap piece of litmus paper.

We cannot be afraid to stand up, as did George Washington's ragged soldiers, and say, "We have had enough." We cannot be afraid to stand up and say that we do not want lobbyists, ad men, presidential consultants painting their own colors onto the flag. We do not want rich men and women running Congress.

On April 11, 1865, in his last public address, Abraham Lincoln said, "Important principles may and must be inflexible." We have been tricked to believe that these principles have been redefined by our recent presidents, fueled by tycoons and fear, when Thomas Jefferson, 230 years ago, clearly spelled out those principles in the Declaration of Independence on July 4, 1776:

We hold these truths to be self-evident; that all men are created equal; that they are endowed by their Creator with certain unalienable Rights; that among these are Life, Liberty, and the pursuit of Happiness; that to secure these rights, Governments are instituted among Men, deriving their just powers from the consent of the governed; that whenever any Form of Government becomes destructive to these ends, it is the Right of the People to alter or to abolish it, and to institute new Government, laying its foundation on such principles and organizing its power in such form, as to them shall seem most likely to effect their Safety and Happiness.

The foundation of our national lives rests on the principles of Jefferson and Lincoln.

Our power is derived from the people and not from pundits who chomp on cigars and roll gold coins between their thick, manicured fingers.

JULY 8

The earth laughs in flowers.

—Ralph Waldo Emerson

My favorite flower is the black-eyed Susan. I am attracted to the contrast of the deep yellow petals and the dark centers. How much like the beauty of women in Bombay at the street markets as they sway back and forth from bean sellers to spice vendors in their bright saris.

Admiring something beautiful is like loving someone from a distance. When those we love are beyond our reach, we wish to embrace them even more. How far would we go on our bare feet to find that person; how hard would we beat our backs with sticks, or sacrifice our daily routines in pursuit of the cherished one?

When I drive each summer to a small cabin in Canada that my parents bought over fifty years ago, I like to admire the wild-flowers that decorate the sides of the road. I do not know the names of many flowers and weeds, but I do admire their colors: blue-purple, king-red, flame-yellow. We are surrounded by flow-ers and by the idea of flowers.

Pierre-Auguste Renoir, the great French painter who died in 1919, wrote that "art is a piece of nature seen through a per-son's temperament." When we are sad, we look to the stiff chrysanthemums for solace. When we are in love, the rose teaches us how to wrap ourselves in petals of delight. In death, the white lilies curve downward in mourning.

As I drive on the Canadian highways, I can always tell from a distance the gathering of the black-eyed Susans. They either stretch out in a ragged line or cluster themselves together at the side of the road like ballet dancers just before the curtains open. I point and call out, "There they are, the black-eyed Susans." The car zooms along at 70 miles an hour—and flowers, grass, sky, memory, and loneliness rush by the window and disappear behind me.

Yes, we seek beauty in museums and admire Renoir's flow-ers and bathers, and prospect for beauty's gold in the little slips of poems we may find in the rough landscapes of our lives, but we also can find beauty in the common day.

Do you remember the sentimental film *The English Patient*? Remember how the opening scene gave a visual delight of the desert floor, the undulating sand as if it were waves of Japanese water? Remember how supple and skin-like the dunes looked in the honey-gold sunlight?

Beauty is created by gently bending straight lines into curves. Release the wind against the flat desert, and we have Arabia. Push down on a stiff piece of wood and we have the hull of a great ship. Follow the straight hands and brushes of Renoir and we find *The Lunch of the Boating Party, Country Dance*, and *The Bathers* (1887).

Where is beauty? In the mirror of a woman combing her hair? In the jingle and jangle of a street fair in Brazil? What face, beauty? What name? Renoir knew, perhaps, though I am not sure that he considered all possibilities.

We can look at a single rose and define beauty in the shape of each petal folding into the next, and push aside the argument. We blame the poets for the confusion.

Beauty? It is confined to the mind, resides in a cosmic disguise, holds credentials in foreign embassies, sits in the hands of the stone cutters.

Beauty? She walks in the sculpture garden and eats lunch at the Belgian restaurant.

To image too hard the outline of beauty leads to discouragement and loss: discouraged that what we imagine is not there, and loss when we give up the dream. It is easier to imagine delight in the world's imperfections, for there we can find the constant beauty that surrounds us.

One of the first things I do when I arrive at the cabin in Canada is to find a small glass vase, and then I step out to the wild fields and gather black-eyed-Susans, my summer harvest.

We collect seeds of hope. They come to us attached to the fur of the fox or bear. The seeds are dropped in another land where no such seeds existed before, then in the days that follow, new plants are composed in the landscape of our ordinary lives. Sleep each night and imagine it is so, and wake to seek a ready field of wildflowers.

JULY 15

A house is a home when it shelters the body and comforts the soul.
—Phillip Moffitt

In 1920, the poet Robert Frost bought a small stone-and-wood house in Shaftsbury, Vermont. He and his family lived there for nine years, during which he wrote many famous poems, including "Stopping by the Woods on a Snowy Evening," which was included in his first Pulitzer Prize–winning book, *New Hampshire*.

A few years ago, this house was opened to the public for the first time, so I, being a former high school English teacher and a dilettante in the writing of poems, decided to visit Shaftsbury. Located on Vermont's historic Route 7A, the little house is surrounded with seven acres, all that remains of the original property. When I drove down the small driveway, I noticed the barn, a few apple trees, the house to the right, and nothing more.

The main building, built about 1769 and a charming example of early American architecture, was disappointing. The downstairs rooms were empty, except for large photographic murals covering some of the walls with bits of biographical information, neatly printed under pictures of a young Robert Frost.

Encased in glass in a prominent position was a facsimile, not even the original, of the poet's draft of his famous poem. He wrote it, after all, in that very dining room.

Visitors were forbidden to investigate the upstairs rooms because apparently there are government regulations about the size, pitch, and width of staircases for public places, and the stone house did not meet those regulations.

I have visited Washington Irving's home in Tarrytown, New York. You can see the writer's desk where he created *The Legend of Sleepy Hollow*. I visited Mark Twain's house in Hartford, Connecticut, and saw his bed, his pool table, and the very place where he wrote *The Adventures of Huckleberry Finn*. The Nobel Prize–winning novelist Pearl Buck owned a beautiful house in Pennsylvania where nearly everything she owned is still there, just as she left it.

When I visit a writer's home, I like to see his hat, or his book, or her shoes, and his or her manuscripts.

I've lived in two houses all of my life. From 1951 to 1977, I lived in the family homestead, the house my parents bought in 1948 when they arrived from Europe after the horrors of World War II. And when Roe and I married, we bought a two-bedroom house in 1977, and we've been here ever since.

My parents are still alive, eating in the same kitchen, plucking the same daffodils each spring, gripping the same, oak banister, with more tenacity than in the past, as they make their way each evening to their room where I was conceived sixty years ago.

In this house where I write, there are paintings that have not been moved from their spots in thirty-four years. Roe and I have raised three children here, cooked over 10,000 meals, washed the same tub about 1,400 times. The seasons changed 136 times. I wrote eleven books of essays in this house, 1,349 poems, one children's novel, and an adult, literary novel, as of yet unsold and gathering dust.

This is the house where our children first spoke. This is the house where I copied some poems of mine onto the basement wall before I covered them up with sheet rock. Squeaks in the floorboards. The schoolhouse clock. Flower boxes. Home.

What I *did* like about Robert Frost's house was the idea that he actually looked through the very windows I now used to peer out of his dining room. I liked that the barn was the same barn that existed when Frost wrote poetry. Some of the apple trees were the same trees in the yard during his nine, most productive years.

After I become an internationally famous writer, after the president of the United States asks me to read one of my poems at her inauguration, after I win a Nobel Prize for literature, and after Roe and I are old and gray and full of sleep, I'll sell this place and make sure that I leave behind some books and some shoes and some dried flowers from the garden.

I'll leave the room filled with bookshelves, carpets, dressers. I'll post specific rules that you are allowed, no matter what the government says, to go up the nonstandard stairs and look around as much as you like, and I'll leave the kettle on the stove so that anyone who visits can sit at the kitchen table and sip from a cup of hot coffee.

And if I don't become famous, well, I'll leave the kettle behind just the same for the new owners of the house because they will like knowing that this was a home for warm-brewed living.

JULY 16

"Good fences make good neighbors."

—Robert Frost

When I was a boy, the only thing that separated our property from our neighbor's backyard was a row of thick lilac bushes and an apple tree. Billy, the kid next door, was older than I, a tough boy who drove around his yard in an old, beat-up Model A Ford.

He owned a wild dog, Zorro, that seemed to like chasing kids like me—and he was an enemy who knew how to throw apples.

The only true communication between Billy and me occurred in the fall when the apples fell to the ground and we engaged in our annual apple fight. For the rest of the year, the lilac border held firm.

We build walls to keep people out or to keep people in. And yet we imagine machines that travel beyond borders and fly into the future, and we envy birds and the wind, which are not impeded by longitudes and latitudes on cleverly drawn maps. I wish we had no need for obstacles between people.

For over fifty years, I have crossed the Canadian and U.S. border at the Thousand Islands in upstate New York on my way to my family's small cabin three hours west of Ottawa. For over fifty years on my return trip after the two-week vacation, the same thing happens at the U.S. border. This summer was no exception.

As we waited in line, Roe, my mother, my daughter, and I scrambled for our passports, as we made a few comments about how few cars were ahead of us. When it was our turn, I drove up to the U.S. border agent waiting in her little glass booth.

"Where do you all live?" she asked.

"New Jersey."

"May I have your passports?"

I handed her our four passports.

"Please roll down your back window so that I can see who is in the car."

I rolled down my window.

The border agent flipped through the passports, looked at my family, and handed back the documents.

"What was the purpose of your visit?"

"Vacation."

"Are you bringing back any purchases into the United States?"

"Just a bit of pottery: a bowl and some mugs."

"Okay," the agent said as she waived us on.

Every year, for over fifty years, it has been the same thing.

Borders, visible and invisible, made of lilacs or of ideologies, have a tendency to enhance parts of our weaker selves: the need for isolation and hostility.

Perhaps, as Robert Frost famously wrote, "good fences make good neighbors," but once, just once, I'd like the U.S. border agent to say to us, "Welcome home."

JULY 18

Everything about him was old except his eyes and they were the same color as the sea and were cheerful and undefeated.

—Ernest Hemingway

Yesterday I grabbed the straw broom, stepped out onto the deck, and began to slowly sweep the leaves and sticks that had accumulated around the picnic table and chairs.

I leaned over as I reached under the table. I flexed my arms as the broom pushed and pulled at the debris. I walked from one side of the deck to the other, and no one noticed. Cars drove by. Children raced down the street on their bicycles. Neighbors carried their trash bins to the road. A sixty-year-old man sweeping a deck on a Monday afternoon is no spectacle.

I once watched a man being shot from a cannon at a circus. I've admired the New York Yankees at the stadium as they performed near magic with a bat and ball. Fire-eaters, weight lifters, men on the moon, these are the people who attract attention. No one is impressed with a sixty-year-old man in fading blue jeans sweeping a little wood deck in northern New Jersey.

Maybe I ought to place myself in a cage at the zoo where a small sign outside the bars states: "Homo sapiens: roams the earth freely, is susceptible to harsh storms, dwells inside various types of housing, sings, talks, and is capable of thinking and manipulating tools." Maybe, then, people will recognize how deftly I can push a broom. Perhaps tourists will stand on their toes for a better view as I reach down with a dustpan and scoop up little sticks and leaves. Do we have to extract an ordinary man from his routine and place him on display before anyone notices?

Last Sunday, my family and I drove to the state aquarium in Camden, New Jersey. We were all impressed with the penguins and the jellyfish, the bull sharks and the sea turtles, but the greatest show-stopper of the afternoon was the hippopotamus.

It was housed in a huge, indoor enclosure about half the size a football field. There was a hill with trees where birds flew from branch to branch. To the left, a large beach spread out flat and clean; and to the right, a deep tank twice the size of my two-story house. Water slowly sloshed back and forth against the wide and long viewing glass.

Nothing was happening, but then, slowly, two black holes appeared at the surface of the water, and then disappeared. What followed was better than a man being shot out of a cannon. This hippopotamus, which weighed between 4,000 and 7,000 pounds, pushed out of the water to its mid-belly, and then flopped back in with a splash that produced delighted gasps from almost everyone in the audience. Then we could see, through the thick glass, the hippo spinning underwater as if it were a lithe otter.

We were all startled that something so large could have such ease and agility. How can a creature with a barrel shape, huge head, and stumpy legs swim, roll over, leap into the air with fluid grace and dignity?

The word *hippopotamus* means "river horse." It is a creature that spends most of the day playing in the water, and spends much of the night eating plants.

Willy Loman's wife, in Arthur Miller's American classic *Death of a Salesman*, pleads with her sons: "His name was never in the paper. He's not the finest character that ever lived. But he's a human being, and a terrible thing is happening to him. So attention must be paid."

At a certain age, we all develop a barrel shape, a huge head, and stumpy legs, and people forget that we once gave our children vigorous piggyback rides up the stairs to bed. No one remembers that we once swam at the local pools like Olympic stars; that once, long ago we drove jalopies, made love, and tossed bales of hay onto the wagon like Atlas lifting his globe above his head.

No one pays much attention to an old man sweeping his deck in a summer afternoon. No one knows that he is still, in his mind and memory, an agile and graceful river horse, wishing someone would just wave across the fence in delight and recognition.

AUGUST 2

The sea does not reward those who are too anxious, too greedy, or too impatient. One should lie empty, open, choiceless as a beach—waiting for a gift from the sea.

—Anne Morrow Lindbergh

I know people who have lived in New Jersey all of their lives and have never seen the ocean. How many of us have never floated on our backs in salt water?

There is a primal lure to the coast beyond the craving for soft ice cream and deep tans. We liked bringing our boyfriends and girlfriends to the beach when we were teenagers, listening to the Four Seasons on our transistor radios as they reminded us to walk like a man, or hearing Cousin Brucie suggest there was no better place on earth than Palisades Amusement Park.

Have you ever built a towel igloo and crawled inside to make out with your girlfriend? Do you remember wrapping your legs around your boyfriend's waist as the two of you bobbed in the rhythmic waves that crashed against you again and again?

How many times did you ride the kiddy roller coaster when you were a child and your father was young, waving from behind the fence as you zipped up and down the small, iron tracks? There he was, in his penny loafers, no socks, his striped shirt, his Bermuda shorts. Dad, cotton candy, and blue sky.

I see old women in straw hats sitting on the concrete benches, looking out from the boardwalk to the white foam and spray of the ocean.

The ocean is the great equalizer, a power beyond ourselves where we feel meek, or shunned, or lonely. In her famous book, *Gift from the Sea*, Anne Morrow Lindberg wrote, "The loneliness you get by the sea is personal and alive. It doesn't subdue you and make you feel abject. It's stimulating loneliness."

I have come to my own reverence of the seas in part because of my father's love of sailing, in part because I love the novel *Treasure Island*. I have come to understand my own loneliness, stimulated by the sea that does not subdue us.

Here is a poem that I wrote this afternoon in celebration of the simplest seas.

The Simplest Seas

Blessed are, yes, the simplest seas,
Down, seaward, salt, the fishmonger, first the seas.
Blessed are the bits of shells, evidence,
Dried claws, a still seahorse, the hermit crab.
Blessed the Chinese kite, dragon, silk,
Wet sand, all blessed, all sun, blessed the
Umbrellas, stripes, yellow, blessed the girls,
Botticelli, waves, or waves of hair combed.
Blessed are the sandpipers, ricky-ticky legs.
Blessed are the children, cork, floating.
Blessed are the castles and green pails.
There is no air lighter than sea air,
No exposed light more exposed than sea light.
Blessed the sea air, blessed the sea light.
Blessed are the dreams, mist, dolphins,
Such flanks, silver backs, lovers to the dunes.
Blessed are the white yachts, rocking, neighing.
Blessed are, yes, the simplest seas, blessed are,
Yes, blessed, seaward, sandpipers, blessed all
Exposed, so much the sea. We return home
With taffy and broken shells.

New Jersey has beautiful beaches with names that ooze wet
sand: Sandy Hook, Point Pleasant, Seaside Heights. The oceans
cover nearly 70 per cent of the earth. We are pulled back to the
coast, some scientists believe, because of our body's need for salt,
pulled back to the time we first crawled out of the seas.

The season of the sea is upon us. Yes, blessed are we,
blessed all exposed, so much, to the sea. Bring your towels and
memories, books and blankets, and make your way down the
Garden State Parkway with your kites and children and green

pails, and may you return home with taffy, broken shells, a bit of sun, and an ocean of gratitude for being alive.

AUGUST 3

I hear lake water lapping with low sounds by the shore....
I hear it in the deep heart's core.

—William Butler Yeats

I was sitting here in this room where I write, working on a new poem, "God of the Forest," when I noticed a slight hum, a motor-sound pitching out from the kitchen. It was the resonance of the new refrigerator Roe and I had bought. It had been delivered the day before, rolled up the front steps by two burly men in overalls and boots and swung around the corners of the dining room as if it were a box of crackers.

Twenty-eight years ago, Roe and I bought our first refrigerator, a General Electric. Whenever the condenser clicked on, it rattled a bit, and then the motor hummed a constant, steady glide of sound that formed part of the background music of the lives we've lived in our little house, as the children were born and bills were paid, as cats and fish died.

In the first stanza of my poem, I wrote these words:

I've been out this evening talking to the trees,
So you would think, if you were hidden in the tall grass,
And heard my conversation as I looked upward.

I didn't recognize, at first, that the sudden whirring sound from the kitchen was the purring of our new refrigerator. I missed the rattle and jingle of the old machine.

I collect sounds: bells, silk skirts dragging on a marble floor, blue jays, robins, the barbaric yelp of raccoons fighting. When I was in Rome, I stumbled upon a small plaza where four jugglers dressed in balloon pants and silk orange-and-green shirts were spinning sticks of fire above their heads, as a fifth man beat a timbrel, a little drum that looks like a tambourine. Beside him sat a fat, straw basket for donations.

> I know the sound of the forest god when he
> Passes above the trees,
> As his robe brushes against the leaves.
> Some people think it is the wind.

Writing poetry is, in part, creating sound from the silence of a quiet soul. We all have the ability to create poetry, develop our magic thoughts into sound. Sometimes, when we least expect it, we think that we hear the voice of our fathers or grandfathers speaking to us from the dead, reminding us to polish our shoes, or to stop by for the afternoon.

> I see the god. He looks like my grandfather
> In beige pants carrying a cup of coffee to the verandah,
> So I speak to him the way that I speak to the geese
> As they fly overhead. I discuss the journey, perhaps,
> The temperature, surely my own desire to join him at his
>   travels.

I like the sound of the refrigerator vibrating intermittently throughout the day. We do not give ourselves over to silence easily. We step into the house and click on the television. The car radio follows us everywhere. The cities clang, the phones ring, the wheels of the automobiles spin a low, throbbing hum throughout the day and night.

Can we stop and listen beyond the din? Can we stop and listen to what the wind tells us?

> Sometimes he stops and looks down, extends his arms
> And says the ocean was particularly blue that day, or the earth
> Continues to spin accurately, and I am assured.

I like the assurance of bells, and my own heart sound; I like the echo of our wandering voices, our mortal voices as we try to find our way. There are many days when I am filled with a dissonant doubt.

> I sometimes tell him that I no longer believe in heaven,
> And he rains down heaven upon my head and I am covered
> In petals or thunder, depending on his desire to comfort me.

The silence of a flower can define all philosophy. Thunder can wake us up and remind us that we are alive. Perhaps heaven is like a forest, and deep within the thicket, we hear an owl or a bear, some grand creature that is undefined, but singing just the same. Who speaks to the gods in the forest? Who believes in the silence?

> So I step into the woods two, sometimes three times a week,
> And call out his name, and he appears.
> Sometimes we speak. Sometimes I wave my hand above my head,
> And he too waves back at me.
> I know why it is that people think that I talk to the trees.

On my way to New York City the other day for a meeting with my editor at the *Wall Street Journal*, I was driving on the highway when a yellow school bus appeared ahead of me. As I moved the steering wheel counterclockwise just a bit, my car eased to the left lane. When I passed the bus to my right, three school girls with smiles and youth waved and waved out their windows. I looked up through my windshield and, with a smile, waved back. For a quick second, I looked into the eyes of one of the girls, and she looked into mine, and then she smiled again. In the silence she seemed to possess a voice of joy, a color of sound, a fury of youth and hello.

I admit that I talk to trees and believe there is a forest god. I believe there is a sea god, and a god of silk skirts and revelry. I believe in the echo of the neighbor's dog, in the god of a thousand voices. I believe in the voice of joy.

I like the sound of tree frogs on a hot, August night. Perhaps the wind is the robe of God brushing against the forest leaves. Perhaps God juggles Earth, Venus, and the moon as he beats, with a fury, on the timbrel, the small drum of our own hearts, as we sit in our little rooms listening to the refrigerator whirring beside us.

Today is my birthday.

AUGUST 10

You can design and create, and build the most wonderful place in the world. But it takes people to make the dream a reality.

—Walt Disney

Some things are just plain United States of America: Norman Rockwell, the Grand Canyon, Aaron Copland, Emily Dickinson, the Rocky Mountains, Vermont, and Walt Disney World in Orlando, Florida.

We live by a set of ideas written on a piece of paper that guarantees freedom of speech and religion and that gives us the ability to farm our dreams and circle the moon.

We are a nation of flaws, living with our mistakes and doubts, but we also live under the perfection of Lincoln's certitude, and under the precision of democracy. We live in a country that celebrates individual innovation and entrepreneurial courage, a country that holds as an ideal a *united states* filled with a *united people*, no matter what they call God or how they embrace each other.

For over two hundred years now, we have been in a dialogue with ourselves, trying to determine through the Supreme Court, and in our newspapers, churches, and schools, how we wish to define matters of human conflict that do not have single answers. I do know that, despite corruption, despite political agendas, despite advertisements, greed, and arrogance, we still have a majority of people in tune with what is good and simple and even holy.

Roe and I spent the last six days at Walt Disney World in Orlando, Florida. We were both a bit drained from our work and family struggles, and found ourselves fixed in a routine that was plodding and familiar. And we both, it seemed simultaneously, concluded that we would like to live in fantasyland for a bit of time, and create a temporary escape from reality.

I didn't expect much: corny rides, expensive soft pretzels, people dressed up like Mickey Mouse and Goofy—and Disney didn't disappoint. The park was replete with corny rides, expensive soft pretzels, and people dressed up like Mickey Mouse and Goofy, but there was also a clearly driven sheen to the place. Call it a corporate mission, call it product management, call it what you like, but I saw, clearly, an underlying goodness about Disney World that defines the American laughter, that gives a people a place to say, "Yes, this is simple and good."

Each morning or evening, it seemed, a crew of people came out in small, electric carts emptying garbage cans, sweeping the sidewalks, delivering ice, and every one of the groundskeepers waved, smiled, said hello, asked where we were from, and wished us a good stay. They all seemed like neighbors.

The gardens at Disney World are beautiful, sometimes whimsical: bushes in the shape of crocodiles or lions; flowers arranged in the shape of Mickey Mouse; fountains pulsating to the music wonderfully exploding from hidden amplifiers. The grass is greener in Disney World than anywhere else I have ever seen. Even the wild ducks seem perfect, clean, and eager to please and delight.

Disney World has extraordinary roller coaster rides, which we avoided. You can fly with Peter Pan, or dare to ride through Captain Jack Sparrow's neighborhood in the famous Pirates of the Caribbean boat ride. When was the last time you drove on a safari and saw elephants, giraffes, rhinos, zebras, and a male lion roaring at the top of a wide river bank? When was the last time you visited the tree house of the Swiss Family Robinson, or rode in Alice in Wonderland's teacups? Roe and I stood in line three times for the teacups.

In Disney's Epcot Center, we took a walking tour through France, England, Morocco, China, and Norway. Two men performed a wonderful, balancing chair act in the French village. We watched a beautiful belly dancer perform to the rhythms of fanciful, alive, contemporary Moroccan music that would make all of us take off our shirts and wiggle if we weren't so inhibited. Musicians from China banged on their drums in coordinated ease, and the sound was far, far more holy and rhythmic than our own beating hearts.

Roe and I sat on the curb and watched a parade that featured, yes, Mickey and Winnie the Pooh and Poseidon, but also young men and women in butterfly costumes, walking in the darkness with illuminated wings. And everyone was waving and smiling, and then the fireworks exploded to laughter and gasps of awe and delight.

America is, sometimes, "Golly gee!" and Tom Sawyer dodging steamboats. You can see a replica of the Liberty Bell at Disney World, fly over California in an IMAX movie, listen to the music of Aaron Copland, or sit in a theater and watch a mechanical Abraham Lincoln speaking about the evil of slavery and the importance of a nation that cannot stand divided.

Walt Disney World is a happy, clean, friendly place that sprawls out each day with charm at the feet of Cinderella's Castle. It is a good place to delight in America.

Roe and I are back in our routines now, which seem a little less mundane, and I have, sitting on my dresser, a picture of me standing next to Goofy with his arm warmly wrapped around my shoulder.

AUGUST 11

I believe in God, but not as one thing, not as an old man in the sky. I believe that what people call God is something in all of us. I believe that what Jesus and Mohammed and Buddha and all the rest said was right. It's just that the translations have gone wrong.

—John Lennon

My grandfather was a general in the Belgian army. His left arm was shattered in World War I. Ever since I knew him, his arm dangled to his side, a lifeless log, my wooden soldier. Brave grandfather. Good grandfather. As an old man, he leaned over the garden behind my house and planted roses.

My brother Oliver could not see. He could not lift a spoon, talk, chew. He had no intellect. Oliver the simple. Fight the darkness. When my brothers and I lowered Oliver's coffin into the earth, one of my sisters ran up the hill, beyond the cemetery grass. I do not know if she cried.

My uncle was a missionary with the White Fathers of Africa. He painted birds on white canvas, sold his art in Brussels, and returned to the children in the Congo with the money. He loved chocolate. He died on a street in Paris on his way to mailing a letter to my aunt. Shhh. There are candles in the cathedral burning.

Sorrow is not tucked away in the envelope of a distant continent. A man I greatly admired recently died, and I asked his son, "What were your father's last words?" The son answered, "My father, he said to me, he whispered from the hospital bed, he said, 'I am afraid.'" The sheets of the hospital beds are made of white linen.

I slowly ran my fingers along Robert Frost's words that are engraved on his tombstone in Bennington, Vermont: "I had a lover's quarrel with the world."

Last summer, as I was climbing up the steps of a wooden observation platform at a wildlife center, I saw, suddenly, a small gray cloud of dust and grit. At the top of the platform, created for bird watching, stood a family of three boys, a mother, and a father, and they were all weeping. They had just tossed the ashes of their golden retriever over the rail, releasing the spirit of their best friend down onto the wild grass. One of the boys looked over the rail and waved. I waved back.

The Jewish tradition considers suffering as a way to infuse hope to the nations of children so that they will be spared. Muslims call out each day, "God is most great. Come to prayer. Come to salvation. God is most great." Taoism offers a path from the womb, through the rhythms of nature, to the completeness of human life. A Buddhist understands the center of the flower. Hindus seek happiness beyond the ordinary day, and Christians laugh and weep with Christ.

I was asked this morning how do I define my God in the chaos of malaria, starvation, earthquakes, AIDS, genocide, civil war, tidal waves.

My God sits in the temple and prays for the children. My God sits on the floor of his mosque, bows to Mecca, and intones, "God is most great." My God considers the glory of existence in a single stalk of bamboo. My God breathes life into the leaves of grass, and into every flower in the raging silence of Zen. My God seeks happiness. My God laughs and weeps. My God is a little boy watching the ashes of his dog mingle with the open air. My God listens to the father's last words to his son. My God delivers letters in Paris. My God helped me lower the body of my brother into the open earth. My God plants roses with his good arm.

God is in the flowers. God is in the mosques. God is Lao Tse, Mohammed, Jesus, Abraham, Buddha. God is living in Vermont, painting birds in Africa, lying on the white linens of hospital beds, lighting candles in the cathedral.

God of sorrow. God of joy. God of mystery. God of hunger. God of birth. God of AIDS. God of genocide. God of chocolate.

My God has a lover's quarrel with the world.

AUGUST 18

No sadder sound salutes you than the clear, wild laughter of the loon.

—Celia Thaxter

For over fifty years, for two weeks each summer, I have sat at the edge of a Canadian lake and listened for the eerie song of the loon.

In the late 1950s, my parents bought a bit of land three hours west of Ottawa, a place where the general store sold Cracker Jack and strings of licorice, and where at night we could see the Milky Way and, if we were lucky, the Northern Lights. Often, in the morning, looking out the bedroom window, I saw the thick lake mist and heard the distinctive, odd warble of a loon calling out into the Canadian air.

I grew up with the loons, and when Roe and I married and raised our children, we also spent two weeks in July with our Cracker Jack, licorice, and loons.

For all these years I have been observing the famous birds, taking notes, keeping track. The males and females look the same, but the female is just a bit smaller. They have a difficult time propelling themselves into the air, but once up, they fly faster than most birds that I have seen.

I've watched a loon sink like a submarine: releasing air from its body and from under its wings, and slowly submerging. During their mating dance, loons swim in a circle and dip their beaks at each other. I've read that they mate for life, and that their fossils have been discovered 65 million years ago.

Yesterday, after work, I was sitting in the living room read-ing the newspaper:

The war in Iraq is still raging.

Scandals in Washington are still leaking all over the nation.

Children are still being murdered.

The telephone rang.

"Dad?"

My son was calling on his cell phone.

"Hi, Michael."

"Dad, I need your help."

"Where are you? Are you okay?"

"No, no. I'm fine. I'm here at Belmar, at the seashore with my friends." Michael is a graduate of Rutgers University and a paramedic, and he still needs his dad. "There's a loon. I think its leg is broken. It's flopping on the sand. It can't fly. I don't know what to do."

I remember so well when Michael was a little boy, and how I unbuckled him from his car seat and carried him in my arms into the house. So often he'd fall asleep when we returned from his grandmother's house, but then he would suddenly raise his small head from my shoulder and whisper, "I'm not asleep, Daddy."

"Michael, why don't you pick the bird up and bring it to the wildlife center. They will be able to take care of it."

"Dad," Michael laughed with great charm. "This is a loon! It's a huge bird."

Most birds I've saved in my life were robins, blue jays, spar-rows. It was funny thinking of Michael trying to wrestle a large, two-foot-long red-throated loon.

"Mike, I'll see if I can't find an organization in Belmar that might help you, and I'll call you right back."

I dialed information, asked for the number of the Belmar town hall, and when a serious, professional voice answered, I quickly explained: "My son just gratuated from Rutgers. He's on the beach with friends and found a loon with a broken leg. He wants to help it."

The woman changed her official voice to a one of genuine delight. "Isn't it great that a young man shows such concern about a bird? I'll connect you to the police station, and they will call animal control.

"Belmar police," the woman dispatcher said.

"Hello. My son is on the beach and he found a loon with a broken leg...."

"What a nice thing for your son to do," the woman said in a suddenly unofficial police voice, the voice of a lovely person. "Where is he?"

"Well, he's on the beach in your town."

"But the beach is twenty blocks long. Call him back, and have him call me so that we can know his location and we'll send out someone from animal control."

"Michael, here's the number for the police. Just tell them where you are and they'll send someone to help the bird."

"Thanks, Dad. I love you."

"I love you too."

I went back and continued reading the newspaper:

North Koreans still building nuclear bombs.

Congress still investigating abuse of power.

Health care still in a mess.

The phone rang.

"Dad."

"Hi, Michael."

"The loon flew away. I can't find it."

Michael and I laughed and laughed together over the phone, both relieved that the bird was okay. Loons are aquatic creatures, living most of their lives in the water. On land they flop around, and their legs twist backward. They cannot fly from the land. They need, sometimes, a half mile of water before they can become airborne. The tide probably scooped up the silly bird and delivered it back into the water.

"Bye, Dad. And thanks."

How nice to hear on the phone, through the mist of long ago, the crazy, loony, laughing voice of my son.

100 rebels killed in U.S. offensive in Western Iraq.

Trial for two in Rwanda genocide.

Locust swarm in southeastern Nigeria.

AUGUST 20

A lot of people ask me, if I were shipwrecked, and could only have one book, what would it be? I always say, How to Build a Boat.
—Stephen Wright

When I was a boy, my father had a dream. He wanted to build a sixteen-foot sailboat in the basement, and sail it on the Madawasaka River in Ontario, Canada.

There were six children in my family when I was growing up: my three brothers, my two sisters, and me. One of my brothers was so severely disabled that he was in bed for thirty-two years. He had no intellect. He was blind. In addition, my parents never had money. All my clothes were from the thrift shop. My ice skates were from the thrift shop. For many years, the big treat in our house was ice cream once a month. In 1963, my mother bought a used clothes dryer.

My father was never sick. He was never late for work. My mother never complained.

When my father was a young man, he like to sail in the wide lakes of Belgium. When he and my mother came to this country in 1948, they gave up their youth and plunged headfirst into earning a living and raising us children.

When I was ten years old, my father announced that he wanted to build a sailboat. He found secondhand wood at the lumber yards, worked extra hours to buy varnish. For a year, he worked in the basement at least three times a night and always on weekends measuring, cutting, sanding wood. He built a twelve-foot mast. He sewed his own sails. He showed me how to measure, hammer, sand, varnish. I liked watching my father use the hand plane as he shaved the sides of the wood boards, building his dream.

That first summer with the sailboat, he took me out on a wide lake in Canada that lapped along the shore of a friend's home. My father was going to teach me how to sail.

During the first lesson he said to me, "Now, Chris, hold the rope. See how stiff it feels? The wind is pushing against the sails, and you are holding the sails tightly with this rope." I felt the pressure in my hands. It was as if I and the sails and the boat were trapping the wind.

Then my father said, "If you are ever in trouble, if the boat begins to tip over too much, just let go of the rope, and the boat will take care of itself."

My father is now ninety-nine years old, and his sailboat is broken, filled with leaks, and covered with dust in the basement. I know that I will have to soon let go of my father, but I know, even in his death, that the ship of my life will be okay because he took me sailing; because he showed me how to work on a dream, night after night; because, in the end, it is not the sails and the wind that matter the most, but the ability to show a son how to handle the world with dreams of grace and love.

My father is grace and love. I think I will try to fix that old sailboat and show my children how to handle the wind and sails.

AUGUST 21

I went to the woods because I wished to live deliberately,
to front only the essential facts of life, and see if I could not learn
what it had to teach, and not, when I came to die, discover that
I had not lived.

—Henry David Thoreau

I could not understand, at first, why I felt a certain loss when I heard that Fred Schweig had died.

Fred Schweig was a local carpenter in the small, Canadian town that my family and I visited for over fifty years. When we were children, the first place we would go when we arrived in the little town was Mr. Schweig's house to retrieve the key to our cabin. He'd lean into the car, wave hello to my brothers and sisters and me, and then he'd speak with my parents about the rough winter, or about the moose he saw, or about the good fishing that spring, and then he would hand my mother the key.

It was Fred who dismantled an original log cabin and rebuilt it alongside the river where we spent our yearly vacation. It was Fred who announced that there were now bears on our property and perhaps we ought to be cautious about picking raspberries alone.

Fred was not a tall man. He wore various hats each summer: baseball caps, straw hats, formal. Fedoras. A cigarette always dangled from his lips. He told stories about bear hunting and horseback riding. He explained where we might find great quartz crystals, and he pointed to a mountainside with pride. "I own that."

As a boy, I always felt that Fred Schweig was like Daniel Boone, a smart, colorful figure who could survive with only a knife and his wits in the middle of the forest. I can still hear his laughter, still smell the aroma of his cigarettes and the smoke from his wood burning stove. Fred cut hay with a scythe, drove a team of horses to plow the land, and liked the taste of crab apples and fresh, wild strawberries.

There was something accessible, and wise, and frightening, and good about Fred Schweig. When I heard that he died, a part of the boy inside of me died because he was an ambassador from the adult world, and a world that is fading: the country man, the man of the earth, the man who knew the names of the stars and could build a house with his bare hands.

AUGUST 22

I would rather learn from one bird how to sing
than to teach 10,000 stars how not to dance

—E. E. Cummings

In the famous Greek myth, Icarus, the son of Daedalus, had it right: there is both great joy and danger in attempting to be bird-like.

Flying with feathers attached to his arms with wax, Icarus flew too close to the sun against his father's warning. The wax melted; the feathers detached from his arms, and Icarus plunged to his death into the unforgiving sea.

When I was a boy, I was convinced that if I opened my jacket in a strong wind there would be enough lift to fly me above the pine trees in our backyard. My father scoffed when I explained my theory, but he did suggest that, when I was on my ice skates, I open my jacket in the wind. "You'll be whisked along the ice like a bird."

What do the birds tell us? Do they mock us with their songs, laughing that we cannot fly? Do they guide us like angels?

The poet William Wordsworth wrote in his famous little poem "The Cuckoo" how the mysterious bird is hard to see, but its song is a reminder that if we try, we might be able to pursue the sweet call in the garden of our youth:

> To seek thee did I often rove
> Through woods and on the green;
> And thou wert still a hope, a love;
> Still longed for, never seen!
>
> And I can listen to thee yet;
> Can lie upon the plain
> And listen, till I do beget
> That golden time again.

But woe to the person who kills a mockingbird, warns Atticus Finch in Harper Lee's iconic novel; it is a sin to kill a mockingbird because it does no harm and just sings.

Woe to the Ancient Mariner in Samuel Coleridge's poem who killed the great albatross. The bird was guiding the lost sailors out of the Antarctic Sea, but the foolish Mariner killed the bird with a crossbow for no apparent reason, and had to wear the dead bird around his neck as a punishment and burden:

Ah! well a-day! What evil looks
Had I from old and young!
Instead of the cross, the Albatross
About my neck was hung.

We really do have to respect the birds, as Alfred Hitchcock convinced us in his horror movie, and as Edgar Allan Poe reminded us, showing how the raven still sits on the pallid bust of Pallas just above our chamber doors and monitors our sorrows and joys.

We can trust the birds. They tell us in their songs at dusk when it is time to sleep, and they rouse us at dawn with their chatter.

The Dodo in *Alice in Wonderland* offered good advice to the girl on how to dry herself after thrashing about in a pool of tears. The Dodo suggested, "The best thing to get us dry would be a Caucus-race." When Alice asked what a Caucus-race was, the Dodo said, "The best way to explain it is to do it." So they all began to run until they were dry. The Dodo proclaimed that all of them were winners—and that Alice had to supply the prizes.

Birds probably believe that they are the center of the universe. The character Big Bird towers over Sesame Street, keeping an eye on things. No one messes with the barnyard rooster. And someone ought to inform poor Wile E. Coyote that he will never outsmart the clever Roadrunner.

I was reminded of the power of birds this morning when I heard the familiar cry of a red-tailed hawk. For the past two weeks, there has been a huge hawk perched in the pine trees, circling the yard, causing havoc in the peaceful existence of the squirrels, turtledoves, and blue jays that inhabit the neighborhood.

After two weeks, it seemed that the hawk had finally decided that it was time to hunt in another location, and a sense of calm seemed to float down once again upon the backyard, but then this morning, I heard that hawk-like screech, screech, screech!

"That sounds close," I said to myself as I stood up from my couch where I was reading. I looked out the kitchen window and there—four feet from the house, standing on the birdbath like a baron surveying his territory—was the hawk. The sparrows were gone. The blue jays were screaming in the bushes. The grackles had disappeared. There was not a trace of a squirrel or rabbit.

The hawk stepped into the shallow water of the birdbath, and walked around regally as if saying to the world, "It is beneath me to bathe here. I will just dip my beak for a drink because it pleases me."

I never saw a hawk in the wild so close to me before. I grabbed my camera and snapped a few pictures. How grand the bird looked in his brown feathers and speckled vest! How confidently he held himself with his curved beak and powerful eyes!

"Get in the drying race," the Dodo suggests. "Read and be kind," Big Bird reminds us. "Do not hurt me," the albatross and mockingbird ask. "We will guide you and sing."

Even the silly cuckoo bird believes that it is worth chasing after his mysterious song.

"I like to drink the cool water," the hawk announces.

I did open my coat on the ice that winter long ago when I was a boy, and my father was right. I did feel like a bird as I soared down the ice, zooming past my sister and the bulrushes under the steady winter sky.

Sing, drink, race, guide, and do not fly too close to the sun. Beep! Beep!

AUGUST 31

*Most of the basic material a writer works with
is acquired before the age of fifteen.*

—Willa Cather

I have been giving much thought recently to the idea of the upland and the underland. For me, the upland was the meadow in Canada where the wild blackberries were fresh, ready for children to pick and eat as they chose.

My parents bought a bit of property in Ontario in the late 1950s, and each summer that is where we spent two weeks: picnics on the grass, reading by the light of kerosene lamps in our small cabin, hunting for blackberries on the upland: the meadow on the side of the hill, just beyond the first stone wall.

I did not discover the underland until many years later, when there was a rumor that somewhere on the property was a hidden trove of quartz crystals the size of my arm. Each subsequent summer, I roamed the hill and open fields, followed the stream, dug in the outcrop of rocks, all in search of the hidden crystals.

We live between the compromise of the upland and the underland, between the clear surface of what is, and the puzzlement of what might be hidden just beyond our reach.

Last week I received a telephone call. "Bobby died."

Bobby O'Reilly was one of my high school friends and, secretly, one of my heroes. He was the first person who thought that I was a smart kid. He was the first person who made me laugh. Bobby was the vice president of our senior class. He was the star basketball player. He dated the girl I had yearned for since seventh grade, and maintained an Irish sense of humor and warmth that embraced everyone who wisely accepted his friendship.

Bobby was tall and graceful. I remember watching the power of his legs lift him up to the basketball hoop, and I cheered each time, jumping out of my seat, always thinking, "He's my friend. He thinks I am okay." Bobby made everyone he knew truly feel that they were okay.

We never really graduate from high school. The creative writing paper always seems to be due; the football game is always stalled because of rain; the prom doesn't seem to fade in washed-out pastels. If Bobby called me tonight and said, "Chris, come on over. We're going to play some basketball in the driveway," I would step into my sneakers and drive right over and not accept that forty-two years had gone by.

I could not play basketball any better than a pelican could, but Bobby made me feel like an NBA star when he passed the ball and shouted, "Shoot!" I would, and the ball would fly above the backboard and disappear into the woods, and Bobby would give me this smile, and he'd laugh and say, "Well, at least this time you hit the woods." And I'd laugh, and he'd laugh, and the other guys would laugh, and I'd feel just fine.

Bobby played a role in teaching me about the underland, that place where intangible treasure rests just for the finding. He was young, athletic, generous, kind, funny.

As an adult, he developed diabetes, endured four strokes, developed cancer, and was about to have his leg amputated. But when he was younger, his legs pushed him up to the basketball hoops, pushed him up above the crowd, above me when he ran into the woods, grabbed that ball, handed it to me, and said, "Try again," and I did, and the ball swooped in, and Bobby laughed, and I laughed, and he and I were part of the underland, that place where crystals hide and boys know that they are young and silly, and nothing else matters that night.

Alice spent a good amount of time in that underland called Wonderland, that place down the hole of the White Rabbit where everything seemed to be upside down. At one point, she said to the Queen:

> *"One can't believe impossible things."*
>
> *"I daresay you haven't had much practice," said the Queen. "When I was younger, I always did it for half an hour a day. Why, sometimes I've believed as many as six impossible things before breakfast."*

Bobby taught me how to believe in impossible things, that such a popular kid could be my friend in high school, and that a boy on the basketball court could grow into a man who loved his wife and two children, and who maintained his hope, wit, and humor during grave suffering.

The underland is a place where we believe exists, where the crystals hang down for our taking, a place where we go when the upland fields are barren, a place where we remember people who loved us, a place where we believe in impossible things, a place where Bobby calls out, "Shoot, Chris! Shoot!"

For me, Bobby is still playing center position at the basketball game over at the high school. There are plenty of seats in the underland, and the tickets are free.

CONCLUSION

...a breathing too quiet to hear...

—Denise Levertov

At one point, all the starlings, sparrows, woodpeckers, turtle doves, and blue jays at the bird feeder disappear for the night as if on cue. Perhaps they are guided by a sudden, diminished sunset. Perhaps they have a built-in clock that tells them when it is time to fly into the brush and sleep for the night. But the rabbit stays. It stands, shakes its ears, and rhythmically chews the birdseeds that have fallen from the small, plastic bird feeder that I fill every two or three days.

Sometimes at midnight, when I let the dog out, I look to my left and there, often enough, is the rabbit, happily chewing the seeds in the darkness. Of course, I didn't realize that a rabbit's most active time in the wild is in the night.

Fairies, fireflies, rabbits, and bears all inhabit the shadows of the night and the shadows of what I remember as a boy— when I could not sleep and imagined that spirits stepped out from behind the trees wearing firefly necklaces or drinking tea with the rabbits and bears.

Children understand creative juxtapositions: goldfish and magic, kites and seashores, castles and sand. So what does a man think when he finds a rabbit in his yard in the middle of the night? I admit I sometimes pretend that it is a messenger, bringing me word that the Queen of Hearts demands my presence at her next croquet game, or that I am Jimmy Stewart with a six-foot rabbit wearing a tie and leaning against the oak tree.

Three days ago, Roe and I spent four hours on the ocean off

Cape Ann, Massachusetts, in search of whales. After one hour on the tour vessel, the guide pointed and called out suddenly, "Two o'clock, there! The spout of a humpbacked whale!" The captain of the ship spun his wheel, pushed the engines to full throttle so that we could speed, at a safe distance, alongside the rolling whale. And there it was: long, black—floating on the surface— then it silently, magically slid underwater. And just before it disappeared, its tail rose up into the air and then slowly slipped into the calm, blue water. Roe turned to me and said, with conviction and delight, "It is a privilege to see this."

"Whales never sleep," the guide said as we all began to look for more spouts of water. "And they have to think about breathing. We human beings breathe automatically, but a whale has to consciously make a decision and think about breathing; that is why it can never sleep."

In the middle of the night, when I am restlessly turning in my bed, when I cannot sleep, all the whales in the world are swimming, floating, blowing air out from the tops of their heads.

"Whales do rest, however, for long periods of time," the guide said. "They float on the surface and take breaths twenty minutes apart. In this relaxed state they do accumulate enough rest. This is called logging because they look like huge logs just floating on the surface of the water."

We saw two humpbacked whales logging. We saw a fin whale, the second-largest whale in the world, swim within feet of our boat and then disappear with its tail extended in the air before plunging into the water.

"A number of years ago," the guide continued, "an old man came to us with a shoe box. Inside the box were hundreds of photographs of whales. The man said that, in the 1930s, when he was young, he loved sailing out on the ocean and taking pictures of the whales diving, floating, breaching, and swimming. He wanted to know if the pictures would be of any interest to us."

In the distance, a large spray of water broke the surface.

"We said to the old man, 'Yes! We would love to have the pictures.' And because of those photographs, we have been able to identify by the shape and color of their tails many whales still living today. Imagine a young man taking pictures of these very whales seventy-five years ago."

Rabbits roam at night. Whales loll on the surface of the water. Old men keep shoe boxes of photographs from the days when they were young and anxious to seek out beauty with their little cameras.

In his famous book *Life on the Mississippi*, Mark Twain wrote about his way of daydreaming: "When I'm playful, I use meridians of longitude and parallels of latitude for a seine, and drag the Atlantic Ocean for whales. I scratch my head with lightning and purr myself to sleep with the thunder."

We struggle in our lives with certitude, but in the turmoil we can try to be playful and to purr ourselves to sleep as we drag the ocean for whales, or transform ourselves into the mad, March hare.

I hope this little book helped to stimulate the fields of your soul at midnight as you continue to make the conscious decision to breathe.